COMMUNAL VIOLENCE AND PROPAGANDA

COMMUNAL VIOLENCE AND PROPAGANDA

KOENRAAD ELST

VOICE OF INDIA
New Delhi

First published, 2014
Reprint, 2020

ISBN 978-81-85990-97-2

Published by Voice of India, 2/18, Ansari Road, New Delhi – 110 002.
Digitally Printed and bound in India by Replika Press Pvt. Ltd.

Contents

Foreword to the second, separate edition

The present booklet was excerpted from my two-volume book from 2001, *The Saffron Swastika: the Notion of "Hindu Fascism"*, viz. chapter 7, or p.720-831. It records a number of cases where academics and the media reported grossly unfairly on cases of communal violence, as well as the ideological mindset and political compulsions that have led to this reprehensible behaviour.

In the years that have passed, the patterns described here have been repeated again and again. In the famous Gujarat riots of 2002, killing some 1100 people, politicians and media outlets have systematically left out the Muslim initiative, killing 58 Hindus before the first Muslim was touched. Till today, they are reluctant to report that in court case after court case, Chief Minister Narendra Modi has been acquitted. Instead, they prefer to commit contempt of court by persistently blaming Modi. They also left out the evidence of a remarkable Hindu self-control: the preceding months had seen a number of Muslim bomb attacks, including on the Assembly and Parliament of Srinagar and Delhi, yet Hindus refrained from retaliating. A few months after the Gujarat riots, a major bomb attack on the Akshardham Swaminarayan temple in Gandhinagar killing 30 Hindus was again left without reply, for the fabled Hindu self-control had been restored.

Naming and shaming

Among the waves of Islamic bomb attacks was one in 2006 on a string of places in Varanasi, including on the Sankat Mochan temple managed by my former landlord, Vir

Bhadra Mishra. At least 28 people were killed in the holy city. Many South Asia "experts" on the RISA list (Religion in South Asia, an association of American Indologists) had lived in Mishra's guesthouse, Amar Bhavan, and they ostentatiously shed some crocodile tears. However, there was a hue and cry on the RISA list when I repeated the same condolence message but adding the motivation of the terrorists: Islam. Sometimes terrorists just strike without leaving their signature, but more often they leave letters or video messages emphasizing that they did it for Islam. It is therefore only a matter of taking Muslims at their word when we name and shame the terrorists' motivation: Islam. But these Orientalists want to be seen condoling the victims of Islam without ever mentioning Islam.

The Mumbai bomb attacks of 2008, killing at least 164 people (not to be confused with the 2011 Mumbai bomb attacks, killing at least 26), received more than usual attention in the West because among the targets was also a Jewish centre. Some Americans had the gall of calling this "India's 9/11", as if India has not been more often targeted, and since earlier, than America. The typical pattern of Islamic terror attacks, targeting a number of different places in a city at the same time, was first tried out in Mumbai on 12 March 1993, killing at least 257. In London, where the underground train system has effectively been the target of Islamic terrorism in 2005, killing 52, you can still take the underground without any security controls; in Delhi, by contrast, Islamic terrorism has struck with such frequency that every commuter at every metro station has to undergo security controls.

In Mumbai, the killing of a police officer who was known for his anti-RSS views was enough for some secularists to make the ludicrous allegation that the RSS had masterminded the attacks. Such deliberate attempts at misattribution are not that rare. In 2004, when the Madrid train system was the target of Islamic bomb attacks, killing 191, we saw our

Flemish expert Prof. Rik Coolsaet (socialist, but in agreement with the Spanish conservative ruling party) on TV pontificating that this had to be the handiwork of the Basque nationalists of ETA. This group is indeed guilty of some terror attacks, before abjuring violent methods in 2011, but on a much smaller scale and without the tell-tale modus operandi, so this attempt to exonerate Islam didn't carry conviction. And of course, further investigative leads revealed the Islamic provenance of the bomb attacks. Note that the professor always hurries to whitewash Islam but had no qualms about (falsely) naming Basque nationalism as the culprit.

Sometimes the facts of the case are respected though a partisan spin is put on it. Sometimes an important phase of the violence, viz. the part with undeniable Muslim initiative and guilt, is obscured. But sometimes the facts of the case are simply misrepresented. In 2006, former President Bill Clinton wrote in a foreword to a book by his Foreign Secretary Madeleine Albright that the Chittisinghpura massacre of 2000, an attack on a Kashmiri Sikh village killing 36, was committed by Hindu militants, when in fact it was committed by the Pakistan-based Lashkar-e-Taiba, as was also admitted by the Pakistani-American terrorist David Headley (born Daood Sayed Gilani) in 2010. Clinton's mistaken view, which he refused to correct, exemplifies the international perception that Islamic terrorism is easily counterbalanced, and perhaps caused, by an equally virulent Hindu terrorism. It is not any non-existent original Western research into the matter that has given Westerners this idea; it is spoonfed to them by the Indian secularists who control the bottleneck of information on India.

"Hindu terrorism"

Misdirection is the name of the game practiced by stage magicians. The media likewise misdirect the attention of the public towards imaginary problems (and other pastimes) to obscure the elephant in the room, Islamic terrorism. A favourite new one is the notion of "Hindu terrorism". At the time of writing, there are in this regard many allegations, some exploratory incarcerations, some press interviews claiming to have made the accused say what even police interrogators haven't been able to wrench out of them, but little definitive evidence. Islamic terrorism is a reality whereas "Hindu terrorism" is still up in the air.

To be sure, it is possible that some combative but desperate and unorganized Hindus have taken, or will take, to a tactic which they have so often seen being used by Muslims with great success. The more Muslims commit terrorism, the more Western politicians queue up before mosques to assuage the community's feelings, and the more Indian secularists prove their resourcefulness by moving Islam's guilt elsewhere. Hindus won't get away with the same tactic, as the opinion apparatus has prepared the ground in favour of Islam, not of Hinduism. It is also silly to take recourse to this Islamic minority tactic when Hindus could have their way through the ballot box if properly knowledgeable and organized. And finally, Hinduism doesn't have a doctrine of jihad and is sparing with violence, so this senseless recourse to unnecessary violence is un-Hindu at heart.

Hindus at the receiving end

In the Muzaffarnagar riots of 2013, politicians visited the families of the Muslim victims, not those of the Hindu victims, while the media made no mention of or gave no credence to the Muslim conduct which had triggered the riots. This is typical, and it is practiced the world over: Buddhists in Thailand and Myanmar have taken revenge for acts of violence by Muslims, yet all the attention is devoted to the second phase of the riots, viz. the Buddhist counterattack, falsely presented as an attack. In the Central African Republic in 2014, Christian militias have taken over the initiative from the Muslims who had first attacked them, but only the counterattack of the non-Muslims against the "poor hapless Muslims" is highlighted. Muslims are systematically portrayed as victims, non-Muslims as executioners.

To summarize: the problem of Muslim violence is real. A meritorious runner-up is the Maoist guerrilla. While Communism has died down in Russia and China, it is alive in various forms in India, including armed struggle. Secularism infrequently also goes violent, as in 1984 when secular activists of the Congress Party killed some three thousand Sikhs in revenge for the killing of their leader Indira Gandhi. Nehruvian secularism is indeed a dangerous and lethal ideology. Christians sometimes also make their mark, as with the murder in 2008 of Swami Lakshmananda and four of his assistants, after earlier murder attempts had failed.

Mostly, the missionaries use subtler tactics, but here direct action was deemed more Christian. PR-savvy Christian spokesmen tried to use the Maoist weapons training of some of the killers as proof that they were "Maoist, not Christian", but the court case ended in 2013 with the conviction of a range of indicted persons, Christians all of them. This murder was especially interesting for its elaboration in the media. In subsequent days, the affected tribals took revenge on the Christian establishment, burning a few churches, and this news made headlines around the world, far more than the Lakshmananda murder that had triggered it. Till today, the riots figure in lists of "acts of persecution of the Christian minority by the Hindu fanatics", while the murder that prompted them has fallen into the memory hole. Notice also how the Christians always insist that "tribals are not Hindus", but in the present context of riots, the tribals have suddenly been transformed into "Hindu fanatics".

So, this rare act of Christian violence confirms a pattern we have seen time and again in the case of Muslim violence: in the media and in urban as well as global public opinion,

Hindus are always at the receiving end. Whatever the facts of the case, they are always construed in such a way that Hindus are guilty.

To an extent, Hindus themselves share in the blame for this state of affairs. No, I do not mean the usual excuses which the secularists and the India-watchers bring up to justify their own wrongdoing: Hindu casteism, Hindu participation in riots etc. Hindus are to blame for the unfair account which the "experts" and the media give of their situation because they themselves have never seriously invested in media and, more demanding, in developing a proper analysis of the forces in the field. In a way, they are reaping the fruits of their own laziness.

What to do

This brief glimpse of the problem of Islamic violence may suffice for now. In the pages that follow, we have mostly discussed the real power equation in the scene of religious violence as well as in its academic and media representation. For now, however, we can focus on the ultimate fundamental question: how to solve this problem root and branch.

For the immediate future, we of course have to support the security forces in combating the terrorists. We should not shoot them in the back while they risk their lives in the defence of society; that is only what the secularists do. But this emergency operation will not address the source of the problem. For that, we will have to uproot the belief system that animates the jihadis: their religion.

The basic mistake with the Islamic belief system is that it is untrue. Its much-incriminated intolerance and self-righteousness follow from this untruth. When Mohammed found that he couldn't genuinely convince the Arabs of his delusion of receiving dictations from above, he imposed his delusions on them and punished all those who refused to genuflect before him and his beliefs. The theologians have seen to it that this remained the pattern ever since.

Mohammed never heard the voice of God or of Gabriel, he mistook an inner voice emanating from his own brain with a voice from above. While Mohammed's contemporaries saw through his delusion, he broke with them and kept on craving recognition as God's one and only spokesman. Islam is effectively a "*folie à deux*" (madness with two) on a billionfold scale, where otherwise sane people play along with the Prophet's delusion: Muslims assenting to Mohammed's self-image. Once the secularists do their duty and make sure that every child of Muslim parents learns the simple secular truth about Mohammed, the root of their attachment to Mohammed's belief system and model conduct will dissolve. They will become immune to calls for jihad.

This is serious business, and should not be made to lose its teeth by the predictable pleas for a "moderate Islam". Muslim leaders have assured us that there is no "moderate" versus "fundamentalist" Islam, but only Islam. Yet, secularists and soft-brained Hindus keep chasing this mirage of "moderate Islam" because of the observable fact that many Muslims don't practice jihad. They are bound to fail the day they try to find a "moderate Islam" in the Quran and Hadith texts in which all Muslims believe; but they are able to point to moderate people who call themselves Muslim.

Who are these "moderate Muslims"? They are people who have only been superficially touched by Islamic indoctrination, so that the universal human layer shines through the overlay of an Islamic upbringing. Their existence does not prove that there is such a thing as "moderate Islam", only that they are but superficially touched by Islam. Yet, they have something in common with the jihadis: their religion. Except for a few converts, all jihadis descend from "moderate Muslims".

For example, most people who converted to Islam, did so under pressure, and only paid lip service to Islam. Yet they raised their children as Muslims, and after a few generations, their descendants really believed in the Prophet's claims. They took Mohammed's little box of poison, they didn't open it but just flaunted it in order to better their own chances in Muslim society, and then they passed it on to their children. This way, the box of poison passed from generation to generation, and as long as it remained closed, the modern secularists would label them as "moderate Muslims". But then, it landed in the hands of a generation that decided to open the box and take Mohammed's injunctions to jihad seriously. That is the complicity of the "moderate Muslims" in jihad.

Add to this the support which Muslim communities give to their jihadi brethren. As Ernesto Ché Guevara said: the *guerrillero* is among the people as a fish in the water. Similarly, a jihadi is among the moderate Muslims as a fish is in the water. So, "moderate Muslims" don't have blood on their hands, but they are not altogether innocent. Mind you, we should not berate them for this, we all are susceptible to the law of unintended consequences; but it remains nonetheless a fact that Islam itself, even in light doses, is harmful. It should disappear.

Ex-Muslims will then turn their mosques into secular buildings, or into temples of their adopted religion. After that, we will have other problems to deal with, no doubt. If people don't have Islam to fight for, they easily find something else. Islam is but one mistaken belief system emanating from the human mind, along with others. Some wrong beliefs cause people to become intolerant and violent, others cause different kinds of misconduct. So, we will still have enough to deal with. But the specific problem of Islamic violence forces itself upon us now, so we have to do something about it now.

If there exist Hindus who think they can solve this religious problem by means of reverse terrorism, they are mistaken. They have a quasi-racial conception of the existing communities, as if there is a race that has always been Muslim and is bound to remain so unless exterminated. Instead, Indian Muslims know very well that part of their ancestry was Hindu once (and their "promotion" to Muslimhood is for them an extra reason for feeling superior to those who have remained in the "darkness" of Hinduism), and that all of their ancestry was non-Muslim once, like Mohammed's Pagan mother. They hope to convert all Hindus to Islam, but instead, they themselves should be converted out of Islam.

At any rate, their religious identity can and must change. Muslims have to discover that they are just normal human beings, no different from the accursed non-Muslims. They should convert to humanity.

DR. KOENRAAD ELST

Mortsel (Belgium), 24 February 2014

1. Communal violence and propaganda

Hindutva slogans and argumentations are routinely decried as mendacious propaganda of the type developed by Hitler's propaganda minister Joseph Goebbels. In this chapter, we will look at a sample. We will also pay attention to the use of data on interreligious violence for purposes of creating and propagating an enemy-image.

1.1. LENIN, GOEBBELS, ORWELL

1.1.1. "The big lie"

When secularists dislike observations by Hindutva spokesmen, especially when they find themselves unable to come up with a substantive rebuttal, they allege that their opponents are indulging in "Goebbelsian lies!" Sometimes they add that Joseph Goebbels, Hitler's propaganda minister, employed the technique of the "big lie". This means that he believed daring lies were more convincing than modest lies, and that all it took to make a daring lie gain general acceptance was its sheer repetition through every channel available.

Armed with this doctrine, Goebbels went on to become the arch-liar, the proverbial propagator of lies. Undeniably, Goebbels' propaganda used lies when expedient, just as it also used truth whenever that seemed to serve his cause. With the state machinery and the new media of radio and cinema at his disposal, he irrefutably opened up new horizons in public opinion engineering. Yet, there are a few problems with the familiar picture of Goebbels as the gold medal in the art of lying.

Firstly, Goebbels arrived too late on the scene to be the real pioneer of 20th-century innovations in mendacious propaganda. He had been preceded by Lenin and the Communist movement, which actually went farther down this road than imitator Goebbels would ever get. Pro-Nazi filmmaker Leni Riefenstahl was but the German answer to Soviet filmmaker Sergei Eisenstein (note however that in contemporary film schools, Eisenstein is studied as a pioneer and Riefenstahl as an aberration).

Secondly, the term "the big lie" was not a deliberate Nazi recipe for propaganda. It originates in Hitler's book *Mein Kampf*, where Hitler identifies lying as the central technique of the Jewish will to power. Quoting Arthur Schopenhauer as calling the Jew "the great Master of Lies", Hitler continued: "The kind of existence which he leads forces the Jew to the systematic use of falsehood".[1] He ascribed the leftist propaganda which brought down the German emperor and "stabbed the German soldiers in the back" in November 1918 to the uniquely Jewish capacity for deceit: "Only the Jew knew that by an able and persistent use of propaganda heaven itself can be presented to the people as if it were hell and, vice versa, the most miserable kind of life can be presented as if it were paradise. The Jew knew this and acted accordingly. But the German, or rather his government, did not have the slightest suspicion of it. During the War the heaviest of penalties had to be paid for that ignorance."[2]

Specifically, "the Jews, with their unqualified capacity for falsehood, and their fighting comrades, the Marxists" propagated the notion that the responsibility for Germany's capitulation lay with the military leadership (an allegation

---

[1]A. Hitler: *Mein Kampf*, Jaico reprint, p.256.

[2]A. Hitler: *Mein Kampf*, Jaico reprint, p.231.

which happened to be largely correct)[3], notably on General Erich von Ludendorff: "By placing responsibility for the loss of the world war on the shoulders of Ludendorff they took away the weapon of moral right from the only adversary dangerous enough to be likely to succeed in bringing the betrayers of the Fatherland to Justice."[4] And that, then, was said to be an application of the technique of the Big Lie, which Hitler explains with a fair dose of pop psychology:

"All this was inspired by the principle — which is quite true in itself — that in *the big lie* there is always a certain force of credibility; because the broad masses of a nation are always more easily corrupted in the deeper strata of their emotional nature than consciously or voluntarily, and thus in the primitive simplicity of their minds they more readily fall victims to *the big lie* than the small lie, since they themselves often tell small lies in little matters but would be ashamed to resort to large-scale falsehood. It would never come into their heads to fabricate colossal untruths, and they would not believe that others could have the impudence to distort the truth so infamously."[5]

So, the notion of the Big Lie was not one that Hitler embraced, but one that he loathed and condemned as an instance of Judeo-Bolshevik mischief. The core of truth in his perception was that the Bolsheviks did indeed set new standards of mendaciousness, standards which even Goebbels would never meet. This correct glimpse was distorted by the choice of a largely correct analysis of the

---

[3]As Paul Johnson points out (*Modern Times*, p.107), "the magnitude of the defeat was the fault of the generals and the admirals", and (p.109) "it was Ludendorff, suddenly aware that the game was up, and determined to preserve the army intact while there was still time, who insisted on an armistice (...) And it was the army, having helped to engineer the war, having raised the stakes and ensured that the defeat was calamitous, which then slipped out of its responsibilities".

[4]A. Hitler: *Mein Kampf*, Jaico reprint, p.198.

[5]A. Hitler: *Mein Kampf*, Jaico reprint, p.198; emphases added.

German defeat as his central instance of Bolshevik lies, and by the identification of Bolshevism and its lies with Judaism. He should have visited Calcutta or JNU to see for himself that non-Jewish Bolsheviks are as mendacious as any.

1.1.2. "Newspeak"

In a paper outlining the basic features of the "fascist mentality", or "Ur-fascism", Italian scholar Umberto Eco asserts that among other typical crimes, "Ur-fascism speaks Newspeak".[6] This is wrong. The term *Newspeak* was created by George Orwell in his famous book *1984* as an allusion to *Communist* language. When the people in his book hold a demonstration to thank Big Brother for *raising* food rations after he had actually *lowered* the rations, this was a very realistic parody of conditions under Communism. In Communist jargon, the meanings of words are often inverted: the pleonasm "people's democracy" effectively means "dictatorship", a terrorist group passes as a "revolutionary court of justice", the army which turned China into a vast concentration camp was called the People's Liberation Army, the conquest of Tibet was the "peaceful liberation of Tibet", a law in China forcing women to have eugenic abortions is called "Law on the Protection of Mother and Child", etc.

In this respect, Communism was definitely worse than Fascism and National-Socialism: the latter regimes used plenty of mendacious propaganda, including euphemisms ("special treatment") comparable to military euphemisms of democratic regimes, e.g. "collateral damage" meaning civilian victims of the American air force's carpet-bombing. Stray bits of this type of spin could be found already in antiquity, e.g. an observer of the Roman conquest once remarked: "They create a desert and call it peace." But those generals and Goebbels did not twist the meaning of words

[6]Umberto Eco: "Ur-fascism", *New York Review of Books*, 22-6-1995, p.14. The German prefix *ur-* means "primeval, original".

into its diametrical opposite. Thus, Goebbels did not label the Nazi dictatorship as a "democracy".[7]

Of course, the Fascist and Nazi regimes were mendacious, but the specific term *Newspeak* belongs elsewhere: in the Communist regimes and in the writings of Communist intellectuals. It is possible that Eco, who in 1995 served as adviser to the Italian Communist-dominated "Olive Tree" coalition, deliberately tries to obscure the meaning and connotations of this term.[8]

All the same, he has Indian followers: "As a participant writer pointed out, the first and foremost attack of all fascists is directed against words — which are distorted beyond recognition".[9] That is historically untrue: Mussolini found himself in power after a mere three years of action and organization, not of ideological struggle and the poisoning of public discourse. His was an action movement, which never had the intellectual temperament needed to plan the systematic subversion of language the way Communism did.

To be sure, truthful language is important, and its suppression by governments or other powers is a sure sign of

---

[7]In the early period, there were a few instances where Nazis and Fascists invoked "democracy" or rather "the will of the people"; but then, it remains a fact that unlike Lenin and Mao, they had come to power *legally*, and had been empowered by duly constituted parliaments to overrule and eventually abolish these same parliaments. Subsequently, and along with many other interbellum political movements and observers, they openly expressed their contempt for democracy.

[8]In the Italian elections of 1995, the leftist alliance called itself "olive tree", as a poetic and politically meaningless counterpart to the rightist alliance's clear self-description as the "pole of freedom". This was a case of rearguard *Newspeak* used by Communism in retreat, and has been emulated by leftists all over Europe, e.g. the German socialists started calling their socialism "the new centre", Tony Blair called his New Labour "the third way" (an old Christian-Democratic as well as fascist slogan), all hiding their agendas in a terminological fog.

[9]Mohammad Hasan: "Ayodhya Revisited — in revealing film", *The Statesman*, 22-1-1993.

authoritarianism (all the more reason not to twist, of all words, the term *Newspeak* itself, Mr. Eco). Where words lose their meaning, people are about to lose their freedom, as Confucius said. By this standard, India is in some real danger, for the elite does use some Newspeak frequently; not just euphemisms or other general-category lies, but specifically Newspeak in the Orwellian sense: words which mean exactly the opposite of what they ought to mean.

Thus, demanding a Civil Code common to all citizens regardless of their religion counts as "anti-secular", while separate religion-based law systems and other privileges to religious minorities are "a guarantee of secularism". When Kashmiri Hindus have to flee their homes after reading open threats in the Urdu papers and seeing relatives butchered, they are called "migrants"; but when Bangladeshi Muslims terrorize their Hindu neighbours and then migrate from their Islamic state to India in search of job opportunities, they are called "refugees".[10]

This type of inversion of word meanings is part of a wider mind-set of mendaciousness expressed through more ordinary lies, often of breathtaking effrontery. Thus, only in the Orwellian world of Indian secularism is it possible to denounce as "vicious hate propaganda" the VHP's factual observation that the Christian missionaries aim for the complete conversion of India to Christianity, implying the annihilation of Hinduism, Jainism, Sikhism, especially when this observation was confirmed by the Pope himself (Manila 1995, Delhi 1999) when he announced a "rich harvest of faith" in Asia.

That the Indian elite has stooped to this inversion of meanings, is a matter of concern: Eco, though a militant

---

[10]E.g. in the caption under the photograph in W.P.S. Sidhu's "Migrant Tinder-box" (*India Today*, 15-2-1993), Bangladeshi infiltrators at Seelampur are called "refugees". For the description of Kashmiri refugees as "migrants", see any secularist article on that subject.

secularist himself, claims that this propensity to use Newspeak is "common to different forms of dictatorship".[11] As an elitist vanguard movement, Indian secularism has indeed always been despotic, using democratic form when it didn't interfere with its hegemony, but willing to discard that façade when necessary.

1.2. ANTI-MUSLIM AND ANTI-HINDU PROPAGANDA

1.2.1. The circular argument of authority

The secularist media establishment in India, manned mostly by upper-caste Hindus with a virulent hatred of their ancestral culture, likes to pose as the voice of Western sanity amid Third-World savagery. To that end, it sometimes quotes Western sources supporting its own positions. Often these Western sources have first borrowed their views on Indian problems from their anglicized-Indian contacts, so that secularists quoting enlightened Westerners are actually quoting themselves. I call this the "circular argument of authority".

Most Western correspondents and scholars in India fraternize with the westernized Indians, feel at home in those circles, get confirmed in their Western misconceptions and prejudices about India (because the westernized elite avidly cultivates the same prejudices), and are extremely unlikely to develop any closeness to Hindu-minded circles. So if you want to over-awe Indians with the authority argument of Western support (sophisticated variation on the claim commonly used by rioters to confer credibility on rumours: "I heard it on the BBC"), you have enough anti-Hindu Western voices to choose from.

A typical example of this procedure is the use which the *Times of India* has been making of the veteran India correspondent from the US, Abraham M. Rosenthal, e.g. his

[11]Umberto Eco: "Ur-fascism", *New York Review of Books*, 22-6-1995, p.15.

article in the *New York Times* on the Bombay riots of January 1993, reproduced in the *Times of India* on 5 March 1993. We will use his enumeration of "lies" attributed to the Hindutva movement as a starting-point for an evaluation of the "Goebbelsian" character of Hindutva propaganda.

Like the *Times of India* in its editorials, A.M. Rosenthal puts the blame for the Bombay riots for 100% on the Hindus, in particular the Shiv Sena. The fact that the riots started with a number of separate incidents of Muslim violence against Hindus, does not stop him from describing them as a "pogrom". Coming from a Jew who lost relatives during the Holocaust, the allegation of a "pogrom" is not to be taken lightly, esp. considering that historically the Russian pogroms against the Jews tended to be one-sided violence without provocation. If it turns out that Hindu violence in the Bombay riots of January 1993 was something else than unprovoked aggression, this use of the term to designate a case of *retaliation against aggression* is an insult to the memory of the guiltless victims of the Russian pogroms.

A.M. Rosenthal sees the following propaganda as a crucial factor in the January 1993 Bombay riots: "Every day 'Shiva's Army' preaches that Muslims are traitors. They were importing automatic rifles from the Mideast for the day of mass murder of Hindus. They were destroying Hindu temples in Kashmir. They were 'pampered' by the central government. They were breeding huge families so that they would be the majority and again enslave Hindus. Secret protocols showed their plans to conquer India once again. All lies."

Let us take a closer look at the substance of these grim allegations.

1.2.2. Are Muslims traitors?

We can be brief in our comment on the sweeping allegation that "Muslims are traitors": of course it is not true that "the", meaning "all", Muslims are traitors. Recent developments have encouraged many Indian Muslims to shift their loyalty from Pakistan to India, as attested by Muslims cheering for India in Indo-Pak cricket games. Pakistan is a totally failed state, where hundreds of Muslims are killed in sectarian violence each year, viz. by Muslims of rival sects, where Mohajir relatives of Indian Muslims are discriminated against, where drug barons and arms smugglers and fanatical mullahs rule the roost. India, by contrast, and in spite of its undeniable problems, is an emerging superpower, an awakening economic elephant, a technological frontrunner, and still carrying a unique cultural halo, topping the travel agenda of cultured tourists from France or Japan or even Egypt.[12] So, post-Partition Muslims are turning away from the Pakistani nightmare and waking up to the reality of India, a fatherland of which they can be proud.

Yet, the assumption that Muslims are under serious risk of a propensity to treason, has not come about without the impact of reality. Elements of Muslim treason are available from numerous anecdotes of Indian history. The most consequential one was probably the reversal of fortunes in the battle of Talikota (1565), when two Muslim commanders in the Vijayanagar army, which was winning the battle against the invading Muslim coalition, turned against their king Rama Raya and utterly routed the Hindu army. Such were the wages of "composite culture", of a multi-religious army.

For modern history, it is often claimed that in the Indo-Pak wars over Kashmir, Muslims have never been disloyal to India; but this has only been true when the Kashmiri Muslims saw no chance of a Pakistani victory. In the 1947-48 Pakistani invasion, many inhabitants of what is now Pak-occupied Kashmir eagerly participated in what became the final

---

[12]Among Egyptian authors, both Naguib Mahfouz and Nawal al-Saadawi have expressed their love for India, their "second fatherland".

extermination of the Hindu-Sikh minorities there.[13] The Prime Minister of princely Kashmir, Mehr Chand Mahajan, sent word to Sardar Patel: "Practically the whole of our Muslim military and police has either deserted or has not behaved in a proper manner."[14] It is no surprise that Sardar Patel kept the Muslim presence in the police and the army down to an absolute minimum.

In the separatist violence since 1989, thousands of Kashmiri Muslims have behaved as traitors to India. The typical story of the Hindu refugees (belonging to the extremely secularist Pandit community which used to pride itself on its good relations with the Muslims) was that their Muslim neighbours suddenly turned against them once the call for *jihad* had been given through the Urdu press and the mosque loudspeakers. Many ordinary Kashmiri Muslims took an active part in the killing and expulsion of their Hindu neighbours in 1990. Many more have given the terrorists tacit logistic and material support and have refused to report on them to the security forces. They were or are the water in which the separatist fish could swim. So there, the facile contrast between the peaceful ordinary people and the evil agitators just doesn't apply.

In secularist writing about the Kashmir problem, the complicity of thousands of non-combatant Kashmiri Muslims in the expulsion of the Hindus, a fact so prominent in most testimonies by Hindu refugees, is never acknowledged, not even in the rare cases where the expulsion of the Hindus is

---

[13]Vide e.g. S. Kumar Mahajan: "The fall of Mirpur", *Organiser*, 4-1-1998, a late report on the fiftieth anniversary. The caption under an accompanying picture reads: "Mirpur refugees sombrely remembering the Mirpur holocaust on November 25, which they have christened the Mirpur Balidan Diwas".

[14]Missive dated 23-10-1947, quoted in Sahil Brelvi: "The saviour of Srinagar", *Organiser*, 18-8-1996.

mentioned at all. Thus, my compatriot Jean Drèze, professor at the Delhi School of Economics, writes about the remaining Kashmiris, i.e. Kashmiri Muslims, as "deeply peace-loving people" who "take pride in their non-violent nature". Nothing unpeaceful about killing and expelling Hindus, you know. Their "non-communal and non-violent outlook" is still there (indeed, given their oppression by "a predominantly Hindu Army which takes its orders from a BJP-led government, it is remarkable that the conflict has not taken a more communal turn"), but it "is in danger of subsiding as Army repression pushes them into the hands of foreign-sponsored, fundamentalist groups".[15]

The attempt to blame the Army has got things (deliberately) backwards: the Army started its "repression" *after* the Kashmiris, led by Mujahedin who were then still mostly natives, revolted against the Indian state and uncommunally kicked out the Pandits. At that point, in 1989, the Kashmiris were the most pampered ethnic group in India, with free education up to Master's level and subsidized prices of the food imported by airplane.

At any rate, even Jean Drèze effectively ascribes disloyalty to the Kashmiri Muslims: "As far as the local population is concerned, Kashmir is 'occupied' by a foreign army. (...) As for the militants, they seem to enjoy various degrees of popular support (...) partly because they are seen to be upholding the common cause — *âzâdî*. (...) the main concern of ordinary people is to be able to lead their life without harassment, and to be free from Delhi's yoke. (...) It is no wonder that the Indian Government's attempt to entice the State into the national fold has failed to strike a chord with

---

[15]"Jean Drèze on Kashmir problem", *Muslim India*, May 2000, p.216, courtesy *The Hindu*, 29-3-2000. So this is what they teach at the Delhi School of Economics: stopping a bus in Jammu and selecting the Hindu passengers to shoot them is not, repeat *not*, communal.

the Kashmiri people."[16] Take it from a paleface secularist: not just the Afghan mercenaries but the Kashmiri Muslims themselves want "freedom" from the "yoke" of Delhi, they are disloyal to Delhi.

In the numerous publications by Hindutva authors and politicians, I cannot exclude that there may be some such blanket allegation against "*the* local population" of Kashmiri Muslims. But the official line now is to flatter the Kashmiri Muslims (Vajpayee surprised friend and foe by inviting their party, the National Conference, into his coalition in 1998) and to blame the foreign mercenaries and Pakistan. Now that the RSS/BJP is eager to court the Indian Muslims, it likes to highlight some prominent Muslim servants of the Indian state, from cricket players to nuclear defence scientists. Such people satisfy a demand made of the Indian Muslims: "Muslims must now convince Hindus of their love for their country and that it is as deep as that for their religion; instead of resenting the taunt of disloyalty, they should try to dispel it."[17]

We should steer clear here of two extremes, viz. the generalization of guilt for Islamic terror to the whole Muslim community, and its strict confinement to only those who are in the pay of Pakistan and have fired lethal gunshots or

---

[16]"Jean Drèze on Kashmir problem", *Muslim India*, May 2000, p.216. With "Kashmiri people", only the Muslims are meant: there was never any question of "enticing" Hindus and Buddhists into the national fold, they are loyal without special pampering. Note that some Hindu secularists around the Dogra royal family used to entertain wishes of independence (as a Muslim-majority state) before the Pakistani invasion of late 1947 forced the need of accession to India on them; ever since, in spite of their collective leftward drift under Nehru's influence, they have remained loyal to India. Incidentally, in what Muslim country would a resident foreigner like Jean Drèze be allowed to blame the Army for terrorism? And in what "fascist" state would he get away with calling the legal government a "yoke", considering that this was published under a "Hindu fascist" regime?

[17]M.V. Kamath in *Organiser*, 7-5-1995.

triggered lethal explosions with their own hands. Numerous Indian Muslims wouldn't hesitate to defend their country in case of a Pakistani attack, and after the fixing of the Line of Control in Kashmir, there have not been any cases of disloyalty by Muslim soldiers in the successive conflicts with Pakistan. In principle, when meeting a Muslim, you should assume his perfect loyalty to India. However, there is a grey area of people who would not go out of their way to practise terrorism, but who do go along in fighting India and killing Hindus once the call to *jihad* has been given, or who at any rate provide passive support.

This explains why agents of the Pakistani Inter-Services Intelligence (ISI) easily find shelter in strongly ideologized Muslim circles in India. In November 1994, in a raid in Nadwat-ul-Ulama College, Lucknow, police "were successful in arresting a confirmed ISI agent, Abu Baqr, from the college premises". The behaviour of the authorities of this famed Islamic institute certainly justified questions about their loyalty to India: the college authorities, "despite being fully aware of the identity of another ISI agent, Khursheed Ahmad, tried to mislead the investigating officers"; police have found out that "as many as four ISI agents had inhabited the Nadwa college during the past few years"; a month earlier, police "arrested an ISI agent hiding" in another leading Islamic institute, Deoband College of Islamic Studies in Saharanpur.[18]

As if to illustrate the clout which these disloyal Islamic institutes have, Union Home Minister S.B. Chavan (Congress) condemned the raid and punished ten officers by shifting them to other posts, so that: "There is considerable demoralisation and resentment among the rank and file of the Intelligence Bureau (IB) following instructions by the ministry of home affairs that it should desist from carrying out

[18]Sharad Gupta: "IB raid brings politics of religion to centre stage", *Indian Express*, 25-11-1994.

any operations against minority educational institutions".[19] This is one particularly dangerous case of what Hindu nationalists call "Muslim appeasement".

1.2.3. Maulana Azad, a model traitor

Before moving on to Abe Rosenthal's other allegations, I propose we look more closely into an interesting instance of RSS "Muslim traitor" discourse. In recent years, the RSS and BJP have strongly projected the Gandhian notion of the "nationalist Muslim" in their campaigns to enlist Muslim support. Yet, in the writings of Guru Golwalkar, we find an unforgiving retrospective criticism of the "nationalist Muslims" of the Gandhian age.

Thus, the most explicit Muslim opponent of Partition was probably the Pathan leader Khan Abdul Ghaffar Khan, but in spite of the applause he usually gets in Indian history books, his loyalty was not to India: "Khan Abdul Ghaffar Khan who is renowned as the Frontier Gandhi has said that his reason for cooperating with the Congress was that Mahatmaji and other Congress leaders had assured him that when the British are ousted, he would be helped to found a separate state called Pakhtoonistan."[20]

This means that Khan was just as much a separatist as Jinnah was, but on ethnic rather than on religious grounds. In the North-West Frontier Province, Khan's projected Pakhtoonistan, the Muslim majority voted against the Pakistan scheme, but once Pakistan had come into existence and embarked on a policy of islamization in stages, Khan and his followers did precious little to protect the Hindus during the Partition massacres, nor to defend secularism afterwards.

---

[19]Ravi Bhatia: "Resentment in IB over instructions", *Times of India*, 2-12-1994.

[20]Golwalkar: *Spotlights*, p.49. I have not been able to locate this statement ascribed to Khan, but it would be consistent with his later ineffective musings (all through the more than forty post-Partition years of his life) about a separate Pathan state.

An even more important example of a loyal nationalist Muslim who turned out to be something else, was Maulana Abul Kalam Azad (1888-1958), India's first Minister of Education: "The other example can be of Maulana Azad. (...) He has also implied in his various observations that if the Muslims had followed him rather than Jinnah he would have made them virtually masters of the whole land, whereas Jinnah was satisfied with only a portion of it."[21] Golwalkar's argument is that Azad was not more secular than Jinnah, merely more far-sighted and ambitious: he schemed to bring the whole of India under Islamic control.

In more detail: "The greatest 'nationalist Muslim' of our times, Maulana Azad too in his last days gave out his mind in the book *India Wins Freedom* in unmistakable terms.[22] (...) he has not a single word of censure for the heinous massacres and atrocities committed by Muslims on Hindus in various places like Calcutta, Noakhali etc. More than all, the entire burden of his opposition to the creation of Pakistan was that it would be against the interests of Muslims! In effect, Azad says, the Muslims were fools in following Jinnah, as thereby they got only a fraction of the land whereas if they had followed his advice they would have had a decisive voice in the affairs of the entire country in addition to all the benefits of Pakistan! Sri Mehrchand Mahajan, ex-Chief Justice of the Supreme Court, (...) says, 'The Maulana was more shrewd than Mr. Jinnah. Left to him, India would have become virtually a Muslim-dominated country.'"[23]

With this, Golwalkar undeniably has a point. A perusal of Maulana Azad's writings shows the ambiguity of his "nationalism". In 1921, Azad wrote that Hindu-Muslim co-

---

[21]M.S. Golwalkar: *Spotlights*, p.49.

[22]M.S. Golwalkar: *Bunch of Thoughts*, p.245. A sharp criticism of the self-serving inaccuracies in Azad's memoirs is developed at length in Rajmohan Gandhi's detailed review *India Wins Errors*, Radiant Publ., Delhi 1989.

[23]M.S. Golwalkar: *Bunch of Thoughts*, p.245-246; no further reference given.

operation was in complete conformity with the Prophet's vision, for Mohammed himself "prepared a covenant between the Muslims and the Jews of Medina. In the covenant it was mentioned that ultimately the Muslims and the non-Muslims would become one nation (*ummah wâhidah*). (...) Thus if I say that the Muslims of India cannot perform their duty unless they are united with the Hindus, it is in accordance with the tradition of the Prophet who himself wanted to make a nation of Muslims and non-Muslims."[24]

First of all, Mohammed proposed friendship with the Jews not as non-Muslims but as prospective Muslims, since they already believed in monotheism and prophethood. That is the meaning of the term *ummah*: not "nation" in an ethnic sense, but the community of believers, into which the Jews were to be included in due course. The treaty was not at all intended to sanction the principle of Muslim-*Kâfir* unity.

At any rate, to present Mohammed's covenant with the Jews as a model to be followed is quite sinister. An ordinary reader of any biography of the Prophet, let alone a Maulana, cannot be ignorant of the outcome of this covenant: within a few years, one of the three Jewish clans in Medina had been chased away, a second one was also chased out, but only after an Arab tribal leader had convinced Mohammed to drop his plan of killing them, and the third clan was massacred to the last man. As for the Jews in Arabia outside Medina, shortly before his death, Mohammed gave them a choice between conversion and emigration, so that Arabia became purified of Jews (as of other non-Muslims) within ten years after the covenant which Azad presented as a model of co-existence.[25] Azad could mention Mohammed's cat-and-

---

[24]Quoted in Rajmohan Gandhi: *Understanding the Muslim Mind*, p.226.

[25]Similarly, the Zoroastrians of Bahrain had been recognized as honorary "people of the Book" in a covenant with Mohammed, but soon no trace of them was left; yet A.A. Engineer (*Mainstream*, 5-1-1991, and *Times of India*, 5-1-1991) presents this covenant as a model for how Indian Muslims should deal with the Hindus.

mouse treaty with the Jews as a model for Hindu-Muslim cooperation only because he was confident that few Hindus were aware of the end of the story, and that better-informed Hindus honoured a Gandhian kind of taboo on criticism of Islam and its Prophet.

In 1920, during the Khilafat movement, Azad issued a *fatwa* calling on Muslims to emigrate from India, a country ruled by Infidels. Like latter-day cult leaders who get their flock to sacrifice everything, Azad had a real impact: "the *fatwa*, supported by others, was obeyed by thousands, who suffered greatly during their trek into, and back from, Afghanistan".[26] He never paid for the misery which his mad decree inflicted on thousands of ordinary Muslims. Soon after, he accepted that India was the place of the action. Chairing a Khilafat conference in Agra in 1921, he explained that the goal of the Khilafat movement did not lie in West Asia: "The goal is our own country. If you do not succeed in your own country success will not greet you elsewhere (...) India is the first goal of the Khilafat movement."[27]

The term *Khilâfat* has a very specific meaning, viz. a state ruled by a successor of the Prophet, a state guaranteeing the imposition of Islamic law including the proper relations between Muslims and non-Muslims. It is hard to see how, in the Islamic framework which was Azad's, saying that "India is the goal of the Khilafat movement" could have another meaning than to project the establishment of an Islamic state in India. Indeed, in his *Maslâ-i Khilâfat* (Urdu: "The Question of the Caliphate", 1920), Azad "holds that the meaning of Qur'ân XXIV:54, 'God has promised those of you who believe and do righteous deeds that He will surely make you successors in the land' to be that there can be no *khilâfat* of

[26]R. Gandhi: *Understanding the Muslim Mind*, Penguin 1987 (1986), p.227.

[27]Quoted in R. Gandhi: *Understanding the Muslim Mind*, p.227.

Islam until such *khilâfat* exercises complete government and control over the earth".[28]

Nehru always projected the Moghul emperor Akbar as a champion of secularism and a model to follow. Azad, by contrast, condemned Akbar's tolerant rule as the near-suicide of Islam in India, and praised the purist theologian Ahmad Sirhindi (1562?-1624), who through his opposition to Akbar's tolerance had brought the Moghul dynasty back on the track of Islamic politics, culminating in Aurangzeb's re-imposition of the *jizya* which Akbar had abolished.[29] Under Aurangzeb's son, who abolished the *jizya* again, and under his successors, Islamic power as well as the Islamic character of the Moghul state continued to decline; at that point Azad's sympathies are with Shah Waliullah who wanted to restore full Islamic rule and invited Ahmad Shah Abdali to invade India and defeat the rising Infidel powers.[30]

Even in his support for Indian unity, what Azad advocated was rather less than legal unity and equality regardless of religion. Leave alone the longer-term strategy, his plan for united India immediately after independence was a confederation of communities, with the Muslim community owing allegiance to a religious head, the *Amîr-i-Hind*, himself a vassal of the Caliph in all matters covered by Islamic law. In Peter Hardy's explanation: "Jurisprudential *apartheid* was to be the rock against which the power of majorities would break."[31]

---

[28]Summary in Peter Hardy: *Partners in Freedom — and True Muslims. The Political Thought of Some Muslim Scholars in British India 1912-47* (a path-breaking study of the "nationalist Muslims"), Scandinavian Institute of Asian Studies, Lund 1971, p.24, quoting from Maulana Abul Kalam Azad: *Maslâ-i Khilâfat*, reprint Lahore 1960, p.10.

[29]Yohanan Friedmann: *Shaykh Ahmad Sirhindi. An Outline of His Thought and a Study of His Image in the Eyes of Posterity*, p.106-107.

[30]P. Hardy: *Partners in Freedom — and True Muslims*, Scandinavian Institute of Asian Studies, Lund 1971, p.22.

[31]P. Hardy: *Partners in Freedom*, p.34-35.

There was little chance of convincing modernist leaders like Nehru of such a blueprint for free India. Yet, its implementation was a very real possibility if it could be presented as a compromise with the Muslim League: instead of Partition, far-reaching guarantees to the Muslim minority concerning everything which affects its communal identity. As Congress president in 1939-46, Azad made several attempts in this direction. When Partition seemed increasingly unavoidable and Mahatma Gandhi in desperation was ready to make the most far-reaching concessions to prevent it, Azad put forward or patronized proposals to preserve India's unity by reassuring the Muslim League with the provision that half of all members of parliament and of the government had to be Muslims (then 24% of the population), with the other half to be divided between Hindus, Ambedkarites, Christians and others. This would have amounted to a state under Muslim hegemony.

In 1942, on the eve of the Quit India campaign, Gandhi and Azad assured the Viceroy's Council that they would be satisfied if power was handed over to a Muslim League Government of a free and autonomous India.[32] The Cabinet Mission Plan in 1946, proposed by the British as the ultimate sop for the Muslim League, promised an effective parity between Muslims and non-Muslims at the Central Government level and a veto right for the Muslim minority. After the failure of the Simla Conference in 1945, Azad himself had made similar proposals to Gandhi, including "parity of Hindus and Muslims in the central legislature and the central executive".[33] Without Gandhiji's and other Congress leaders' knowing, Congress president Azad assured the Cabinet Mission negotiators that he would get the plan accepted by the Congress (but didn't succeed).[34] Jinnah

---

[32]R.C. Majumdar: *Struggle for Freedom*, p.695-696.

[33]Ian Henderson Douglas: *Abul Kalam Azad*, p.297.

[34]I.H. Douglas puts it diplomatically (*Abul Kalam Azad*, p.301): "Gandhi was shocked at Azad's informal initiatives vis-à-vis the mission."

never accepted such seemingly tempting offers because he didn't believe that the Hindu majority would follow the Congress leaders in this undemocratic project.

After Independence, Azad retained his position of trust in Nehru's inner circle, to the extent that "secularism" as India's new state ideology was in fact moulded by the Nehru-Azad tandem. Indeed, the basic postulate of Nehruvian secularism was enunciated by Azad in his presidential address at the 1940 Congress session: "It was India's historic destiny that many human races and cultures and religions should flow to her, and that many a caravan should find rest here (...) One of the last of these caravans was that of the followers of Islam. This came here and settled here for good. We brought our treasures with us, and India too was full of the riches of her own precious heritage. We gave her what she needed most, the most precious of gifts from Islam's treasury, the message of human equality. Full eleven centuries have passed since then. *Islam has now as great a claim on the soil of India as Hinduism.*"[35] This one last sentence is the central claim which unites Nehruvian secularists and Indian Muslims but offends Hindus.

Sri Aurobindo agreed with Golwalkar's suspicion of the long-term plans of the "nationalist Muslims": "Does Jinnah want unity? What he wants is independence for Muslims and if possible rule over India. That is the old spirit. (...) Of course there may be some Muslims who are different, more nationalistic in outlook: even Azad has his own terms, only he sees Indian unity first and will settle those terms afterwards."[36] Azad was loyal to India's territorial integrity, but a traitor to its civilization.

Golwalkar's skeptical view of the Congress Party's "showboy nationalist Muslims" was confirmed by a liberal Muslim author, Hamid Dalwai: "What was the difference between Jinnah and the nationalist Muslims? While Jinnah

---

[35]Quoted in R. Gandhi: *Muslim Mind*, p.237.

[36]Aurobindo (1940): *India's Rebirth*, p.222.

wanted a separate state, the nationalist Muslims wanted the whole of India. Jinnah knew that it was impossible to get the whole of India, and therefore he settled for Pakistan. Many nationalist Muslims believe that a *jehad* against the Hindus would have got a much larger reward."[37]

The "nationalist Muslims" (exceptions in Nehru's circle, like Rafi Ahmad Kidwai, notwithstanding) were generally no less hostile to the Hindus, or at least to Hinduism, than the Pakistan party. After all, the anti-Partition group in the Muslim intelligentsia not only included people like Azad who could pass as secularists by virtue of their Congress membership, but also outspoken Islamic radicals like Maulana Abul-Ala Maududi, one of the fathers of modern "fundamentalism", who was to openly encourage terror against the Ahmadiya "heretics" in Pakistan in 1953.

Maulana Husain Ahmad Madani (1879-1957), the other great "nationalist" *Alim* beside Azad, declared in so many words that the Pakistan scheme had to be rejected because it would prevent the Hindus from becoming Muslim, while Hindu-Muslim unity would "bring people to the fold of Islam".[38] He said to a meeting of anti-Pakistani Ulama just before the decisive pre-Partition elections of 1945: "Non-Muslims (...) are the field of action of 'tabligh' of Islam and form the raw material for this splendid activity. Today, by propagating hatred towards the Hindus, this field is being closed and this material wasted."[39] So, he had a dynamic vision of a united India embarking on a process of full islamization, — hardly the "nationalism" of Golwalkar or even of Gandhi.

Azad himself, in his admonitions to the Indian Muslims (as opposed to his speeches and letters to Hindu and secular

---

[37]H. Dalwai: *Muslim Politics in Secular India*, Hind Pockets, 1968, p.62.

[38]M. Madani to M. Abdul Bari Nadwi, quoted in Iqbal Narain: *Secularism*, p.133. *Alim* (pl. *Ulemâ*) = Islamic scholar of religion and law.

[39]M. Madani, quoted in Iqbal Narain: *Secularism in India*, Classic Publ., Jaipur 1995, p.133. *Tablîgh*: propaganda of Islam.

audiences), frequently spoke in terms of "being the strongest", "victory" and the like, e.g. after Partition he said to a demoralized Muslim gathering in Delhi's Jama Masjid: "Do not fear and do not grieve, and you will indeed gain the upper hand if you are possessed of true faith."[40] Though Rajmohan Gandhi and other secularists have no difficulty in digging up sincere-sounding professions of Hindu-Muslim unity for the gallery in Azad's work, there is definitely also a more adversarial side to Azad's view of Hindu-Muslim relations.[41]

The subject calls for closer study, but as a rough generalization, we may understand the inter-Muslim Pakistan controversy as follows. The Pakistan movement sprang from the modernizing tendency centred around the Aligarh Muslim University, which was aware of modern trends like democracy and therefore accepted that the Muslim minority would have to settle for either a minority position or a separate state. By contrast, the so-called nationalist Muslims, known with a *pars pro toto* as the "Deoband school", after the theological academy Dar-ul-Uloom in Deoband, still believed in the relevance of models set in 7th-century Medina or 9th-century Baghdad. No modernist notions like secular citizenship and democracy came in the way of their envisaging a restoration of the Muslim community to its rightful position of dominance in the whole of India. In the Sultanate period, the Muslims were a much smaller minority than in the 20th century, yet theirs was an Islamic empire; theologians well-grounded in Islamic doctrine and history were convinced that this could be done once more.

The more intelligent ones among them, most of all

---

[40]Quoted in R. Gandhi: *Muslim Mind*, p.249.

[41]See Rajmohan Gandhi: *India Wins Errors*, a critique of the errors (mostly in a self-flattering sense) in Abul Kalam Azad's memoirs, *India Wins Freedom*; in the concluding part, Gandhi nonetheless upholds the memory of Azad as an exemplary nationalist Muslim who stood for Hindu-Muslim unity.

Maulana Azad, sought to achieve this goal in a phased and unconspicuous way, through cooperation with Gandhi and Nehru. Guru Golwalkar was generally right in suspecting that Maulana Azad had the Muslim rather than the national interest at heart. For most RSS leaders, though, the case of Azad is hard to comprehend, for in their nationalistic outlook, they can place the phenomenon of Muslims being loyal to a foreign state such as Pakistan, but not that of Muslim loyalty to a non-statal entity like the Islamic Ummah or to a disincarnate Caliphate. It is consequently not uncommon for RSS authors to repeat the Nehruvian propaganda of Azad being a "nationalist Muslim" and an example for other Muslims to follow. On this point, at least, Guru Golwalkar was more clear-sighted than his successors.

1.2.4. The ISI factor

According to A.M. Rosenthal, this is what Hindus were made to believe about their Muslim neighbours in the run-up to the Bombay riots: "They were importing automatic rifles from the Mideast for the day of mass murder of Hindus. Secret protocols showed their plans to conquer India once again."

Any specific allegation about Muslims smuggling arms into India at a given time and place may or may not be "propaganda", but the general allegation that Muslim militants are bringing arms into India is definitely true. In most cases they are supplied by the Pakistani secret service ISI which has a one-point programme of destabilizing India. Just a few weeks after writing the above, Rosenthal must have heard about the Bombay bomb blasts of 12 March 1993. They took place during and just after Friday prayer: timed and located to avoid killing Muslims, they killed hundreds of people, mostly Hindus. If the January riots had made more Muslim than Hindu victims, the balance was restored in one stroke.

After the demolition of the Babri Masjid, the government banned the Kerala-based militant group Islamic Sevak Sangh, along with some Hindu organizations. But while the courts quashed the ban on the RSS as illegal, the ban on the ISS was upheld, because the police had incontrovertible proof of its terrorist designs. Though Congress and CPI(M) politicians had thus far prevented any police action against the ISS, the police was well aware of the nature of ISS activities, but it was still surprised at finding just how copious and sophisticated the ISS arsenal was. Now, unlike the country-made bombs which feature so prominently in ordinary communal riots, the ISS weaponry was imported from abroad. Even government sources did not hesitate to point at Pakistan's secret service as the source.

Yes, Mr. Rosenthal, "they were importing automatic rifles" and much else "for the day of mass murder of Hindus". Friday 12 March 1993 was one such day. With intervals of a few weeks, two more bomb blasts, one involuntary in the bomb-maker's own apartment in Calcutta, and one targeting the RSS local headquarters in Madras, highlighted the extent to which Muslim militants were arming themselves; in the same period, on 26 February, an Islamic bomb ripped open four floors on the undeground parking of the World Trade Center in New York.[42] Since then, a number of BJP MLAs and office-bearers of the Hindu Munnani (a Tamil affiliate of the RSS) have been killed. Another spectacular occasion of imported explosives in action was the bomb attack against L.K. Advani in Coimbatore in February 1998, killing over fifty BJP activists.

No "secret Protocols" are needed to "show their plans to conquer India once again". Islamic strategists are fairly open about their plans. It started with the Quran (39:74), which describes how Muslims will thank Allah on Judgment Day for giving them not only heaven, but the whole earth as well.

---

[42]"Bomb explosions rock New York, Bombay, Calcutta: over 400 killed, 1300 injured (...) mastermind Memon flees to Dubai, then to Saudi Arabia; 76 killed in Calcutta, 26 in Sealdah; (...) US citizens getting 'taste' of Islamic terrorism right at home", *The India Times* (Washington DC), 31-3-1993.

From Mohammed via the Islamic law codifiers and Ibn Taymiyah down to Maulana Maudoodi, Sir Mohammed Iqbal and Ayatollah Khomeini, the Islamic position has always been that "all lands belong to the Muslims because they belong to their God". Co-existence with non-Islamic states is only a temporary condition in preparation of their inevitable incorporation into the Islamic empire. That is not the cranky proposal of a stray "fundamentalist", but the official position of Islamic theology.

Though one can smile about this combative theology when looking from a distance, India as a targeted frontline state had better take notice: Pakistan has the conquest of Kashmir on its agenda for the short term, and in preparation of future acquisitions it supports every possible trouble-maker in India with weapons, money and logistic support. Even ungrateful Bangladesh, which owes its existence to India, has now resumed its role as Pakistan's (or at least Islam's) second front against India. And the weak "Hindu" kingdom of Nepal has become another launching-pad of Islamic attacks on India, as in the hijacking of an Air India airplane in December 1999.

The Pakistani hand behind violence in India is frequently mentioned by reporters, intelligence agents and non-Hindutva politicians, e.g.: "Pakistani drug money aiding militants in India, says CIA"[43]; "ISI-engineered sabotage in Assam likely"[44]; "A Pakistani plan to blow up four buildings in the capital is foiled"[45]. I have purposely chosen titles from secularist papers and from the period in which Rosenthal wrote his article; but similar titles can be spotted till today in any Indian paper at least once a week, e.g. "'ISI hand' in train blasts"[46]; "ISI-funded gang busted in Bihar"[47]; "The terror

[43]*Statesman*, 25-2-1993.

[44]*Times of India*, 23-12-1992.

[45]*Sunday*, 14-2-1993.

[46]*Indian Express*, 23-1-1994.

[47]*Times of India*, 4-5-1994.

network: exposing the role of Pakistan's ISI in India"[48]; "ISI sets up schools to train smugglers"[49].

Everybody knows it: "Pakistan has been infiltrating into J&K mercenaries armed and trained by it to sustain an insurgency of which the local population is getting increasingly tired. Elsewhere, terrorists equipped and trained by Pakistan's Inter-Services Intelligence (ISI), which is masterminding the proxy war against India, are taking a steady toll of human life and causing heavy loss to property."[50] True, the RSS with its lack of an intellectual culture sometimes relies on rumours, but ISI subversion in India is hardly a rumour: "The ISI's involvement in acts of terrorism in this country's border states has been well-documented and proved to the hilt."[51] Government agencies continually run into the ISI factor when investigating terrorism: "The government has some information regarding a Pakistan-aided project known as K-2 to balkanise India by involving communal sections of the minority community in the country."[52]

There is plenty of hard evidence, e.g.: "Following the Bombay blasts on March 12, 1993 in which over 200 were killed, investigations disclosed that nearly 1800 kgs of RDX and a large number of AK-4 and 56 rifles, pencil detonators etc. had been landed by Pakistan on the West Coast of India earlier. In the subsequent months, the ISI was able to penetrate the heartland of India, dump arms, ammunition and explosives at various locations across the country and recruit committed young men from as far places as Trivandrum, Hyderabad, Patna, Aligarh, Lucknow etc."[53]

---

[48]Cover story by Sarita Rani in *Sunday*, 5-11-1995.

[49]*Indian Express*, 24-9-1994.

[50]Hiranmay Karlekar: "Trivia in a time of war", *Pioneer*, 10-3-2000.

[51]"Subversion as policy", editorial, *Indian Express*, 26-11-1994.

[52]"Pak aiding project to balkanise India", *Indian Express*, 5-3-1993.

[53]"India under siege", *Hindustan Times*, 5-1-1996, quoted by V.P. Bhatia in *Organiser*, 7-4-1996.

And it is not only in India that the ISI organizes acts of terrorism. To quote from the Pakistani press, after a series of bomb blasts killed and maimed a number of people in Paris: "France blames Pakistan for blasts"[54]; "Hunt for Paris bomb blasts 'suspects' in City [= Lahore]".[55] And from where did terrorists go all the way to Islamabad to blow up the Embassy of Egypt, a moderate Muslim country which has betrayed Islam by making peace with Israel?[56] Even in the bomb blast at the World Trade Center in New York, there was a Pakistani hand. And Abe Rosenthal wants us to believe that Pakistani terrorists who organize bomb attacks in distant France and even in the US (to which they owe so much), would somehow spare arch-enemy India?

Westerners who are in the habit of identifying Islam with the Middle East, fail to understand the central place of India as a hate object for Muslims worldwide, on a par with Israel: "India is the biggest adversary of Islam", according to Sheikh Mohammed Nazim Naqshabandi, a Turkish maulana, speaking at a *tablighi* conference in Lahore.[57]

The contrast between Islamic terrorism and the Hindu movement is striking. Though some Hindu groups dream of restoring "undivided India", they do not have armed militants inside Pakistan and Bangladesh. Even inside India, their level of "militancy" is quite amateurish. Though RSS workers practise stick-fighting as part of their daily training, they are

---

[54]*The News*, Lahore, 3-10-1995, reproduced in *Kashmir for Kashmiriat: Islamic Republic of Pakistan, Nursery for Terrorists and University for Super-Terrorists*, Delhi 1996, p.28.

[55]*The Nation* (Lahore), 11-11-1995, reproduced in *Kashmir for Kashmiriat: Islamic Republic of Pakistan, Nursery for Terrorists and University for Super-Terrorists*, p.29.

[56]"Egyptian Embassy in Islamabad blown up. 16 killed, 59 injured as suicide-bomber explodes van inside the building", *The Nation*, 20-11-1995, reproduced in *Kashmir for Kashmiriat: Islamic Republic of Pakistan, Nursery for Terrorists and University for Super-Terrorists*, p.31.

[57]The conference took place on 19/1/1993, and was reported on by V.P. Bhatia in *Organiser*, 21/2/1993.

illiterates in modern weaponry. When the RSS, described by its enemies as "the world's largest private militia", was specifically targeted by the Khalistani separatists in Panjab, and hundreds of RSS-BJP men got killed, there was no armed retaliation at all. Here again, one would expect "fascism" to be made of sterner stuff.

1.2.5. The Protocols are in our midst

If the allegation that "Muslims are traitors" is a bit too sweeping to allow for a precise assessment, each of the subsequent claims cited by Rosenthal has a considerable grain of truth in it, as we shall demonstrate. Before going into the details, let us quote one more observation by Rosenthal: "Hindu hate literature against Indian Muslims is almost exactly the same in manufactured paranoia as the *Protocols of the Elders of Zion*, Hitler's favourite, which is distributed still by Muslims in the Middle East and on 42nd Street in New York City." He could have added that the *Protocols* are still quoted in earnest in South-Asian Muslim media like the Jamaat-i Islami weekly *Radiance* (Delhi), the quarterly *Islamic Order* (Karachi), or the anti-Hindu fortnightly *Dalit Voice* (Bangalore). When alleging that an imitation of the *Protocols* is being practised by the Shiv Sena, it is indeed fair to point out that the original is still available in large numbers from Islamic publishing-houses in East and West alike. But does the Hindu propaganda really echo the *Protocols*?

The central grievance against the Indian Muslims is, in Rosenthal's words, "the partition of the Indian subcontinent and the creation of Muslim Pakistan — seen by so many Hindus as an act of Muslim treachery". Indeed, no amount of history rewriting can alter the fact that India was partitioned (over nearly a million dead bodies) under Muslim pressure, and that what was carved out of India was an Islamic state. And no amount of hermeneutics can interpret this as an act of loyalty towards India. From the viewpoint of pluralistic and democratic India, the 93% Muslim voters just before

Independence who voted for the Muslim League with its one-point programme of partitioning India and creating Pakistan, were effectively traitors.

Nothing about this central grievance, which is fully rooted in historical reality and owes nothing at all to mendacious propaganda, has a parallel in Nazi anti-Jewish propaganda. The Jews had never partitioned Germany, nor carved a state for themselves out of it, nor practised ethnic cleansing in that carved-out state of their own, nor reduced the non-Jews to third-class citizens there. The points of anti-Muslim rhetoric which Rosenthal has quoted, can be gathered from impeccable sources: history books, demographic statistics, Islamic leaders' own policy statements, and the text of the Indian, Pakistani and Bangladeshi laws and Constitutions. I am sure Rosenthal would not say the same thing for Nazi anti-Jewish propaganda. The fact of Pakistan can be verified on any world map, its Islamic character can already be deduced from its green-and-crescent flag. Well-attested facts may not be a valid reason for rioting, but they are certainly different from "Goebbelsian propaganda".

1.2.6. "Muslims breed like rats"

The classic example of supposedly Goebbelsian Hindu propaganda is the claim that Muslims have a higher birth rate, and that they will overtake the Hindus numerically in the near future. Or in Rosenthal's words: "They are breeding huge families so that they would be the majority and again enslave Hindus." I have it from a number of Muslims personally, in India as well as in Europe and North America, that the intention of increasing Muslim power through a high birth rate really exists: they say that they are told by their imams not to participate in birth control programmes. "We cannot take over this country by force, so we must do it by increasing our numbers through a high birth rate and immigration": these are the words of Muslim leaders both in Brussels and in New York, or so at least I am told by Muslims living there.

But I will not ask the reader to believe any hearsay. While *intentions* are hard to demonstrate, at least the *fact* of the higher Muslim birthrate can be established very firmly through official data. Like every other country where Muslims and non-Muslims co-exist, India has a considerably higher Muslim birth rate. Ever since regular census operations were started, the percentage of Muslims has grown every decade in British India, independent India, Pakistan and Bangladesh (the only *seeming* exception is Pakistan between 1971 and 1981, due to the reclassification of Ahmadiyas as non-Muslims in 1974). In the subcontinent, Muslims were about 19% in 1881, about 24% at the time of Partition, and about 30% today. Their percentage has consistently increased, with the rate of increase itself increasing. In the fifty years between 1941 and 1991, their percentage (not to speak of absolute figures) has risen substantially more than in the sixty years between 1881 and 1941. In truncated India, Muslim population has officially grown 2.7% in forty years (from 9.9% to 12.6% in 1951-91, not counting the numerous Bangladeshi illegals who thought it wiser to avoid the census operations)[58], and Muslim leaders claim that the true figure of Muslim population is about 3% higher.

The subcontinental total shows a faster growth than the official figures for the Indian republic, and should be considered the more important indicator for the long-term evolution, considering the increasing spill-over of population surplus from Pakistan and esp. Bangladesh. In Pakistan and

[58]Bangladeshi settlers still cannot believe their eyes at seeing India's indulgence of their own presence. Their experience with illegal immigration is that Saudi Arabia locks up illegal immigrants (often overstaying on a Hajj passport) on a harsh regime before bringing them to the airport in chains and sending them back to Bangladesh; that during a recent economic slump, Malaysia threw out both legal and illegal Bangladeshi guest workers; and that Bangladesh itself mistreated the Rohingya Muslim refugees (genuine refugees) and sent them back to Myanmar.

Bangladesh, the Muslim percentage has continually increased, partly by pestering the non-Muslims out, partly by conversions under pressure (pressurizing people to marry their daughters to Muslims, allocating jobs on conditon of conversion, etc.), and partly by higher birth-rates. In Sri Lanka, Islam is growing by demographic means. In Nepal, demographics is helped by massive Bangladeshi immigration; not that massive on the Bangladeshi scale, but sufficient to change the composition of Nepal's small population drastically.

Now, every decade the Muslim percentage in the Subcontinent increases by more than 1%, with the rate of increase itself increasing. In the 1880s, South-Asian Muslims became 1 in 5 of the total population, around 1950 they were 1 in 4, and before long they will be 1 in 3. Already, militant Muslims are talking of Akhand Bharat, a kind of re-unification, and especially Bangladesh suggests that there should be an open border. The perspective of numerically overtaking the Hindus at least in parts of India is beckoning.

That the high Muslim birthrate is intentional and bound up with Islam itself, and not with extraneous factors such as "Muslim poverty", is indicated by a number of well-known and easily verifiable facts.[59] Within the Muslim world, the countries with the lowest birth rates, and the only ones approaching India's reduced birth rate, are the most secularized ones, viz. Turkey and Indonesia. In India, within each class defined by income level, Muslims have a higher birthrate and a lower tendency to practice birth control as compared with non-Muslims. Thus, the Scheduled Castes have, with effort, realized a much lower birth rate than the poorest classes among Muslims, and even lower than the Muslim average, i.e. including rich Muslims who ought to

---

[59]More details in Koenraad Elst: *The Demographic Siege*, Voice of India, Delhi 1998.

have fewer children according to the "not religion but poverty" school. It is precisely among the richest classes that the contrast between large Muslims families and two-child Hindu families (not to mention the numerous unmarried and childless Hindu career women) is most striking. Saudi Arabia has almost the highest per capita income in the world, and still has one of the highest demographic growth rates.

1.2.7. Destruction of temples in Kashmir

One of the Hindu fabrications poisoning communal relations is, according to Rosenthal, the claim that Muslims "were destroying Hindu temples in Kashmir". The story behind this allegation is that after the demolition of the Babri Masjid, L.K. Advani had remarked that much less attention had been given to the destruction of Hindu temples in Kashmir. When challenged on this point, BJP officials published a list of 40 temples in Kashmir, claimed to be seriously damaged. Investigation by Kashmiri separatism advocate B.G. Verghese showed that in many cases, the claim was exaggerated or simply untrue. Not so nice, but what does it prove?

In the first place, it proves the complete incompetence of Hindutva politicians in polemical or generally in intellectual matters. Collecting and analyzing information is just not part of the training of an RSS man.

But it does not prove that Advani had made a false claim about temple vandalization by Islamic militants in Kashmir. The case made against him by B.G. Verghese, who claimed to have inspected the temples listed and found most of them intact, was seriously flawed, as even a paper strongly sympathetic to Verghese was forced to admit: "However, the *Panun Kashmir* [a Kasmiri Pandit refugee organization] declared the report 'an absolute falsehood' and said that Mr. B.G. Verghese, the ex-editor of *Indian Express* and known for his forthright and impartial stand on issues, was 'not an authority to determine' the issue. They argue that he was in Kashmir for only two days and did not venture beyond Srinagar."[60]

In the course of the debate, a few RSS-sympathizing intellectuals (e.g. Dinanath Mishra, who testified that on the occasion of earlier temple destructions in Kashmir, Verghese as *Indian Express* editor had suppressed this news) got their act together, and came up with a more reliable list of temple destructions in Kashmir covering the entire period of the insurrection until spring 1993.[61] The campaign of destruction did not stop then, of course.

If mistakes were made about the destruction of temples in Kashmir, it is best to keep in mind that these instances of temple destruction were a small matter when compared with similar incidents in Pakistan and Bangladesh. A list of hundreds of temples destroyed in Bangladesh in 1989 alone was compiled by the Hindu-Christian-Buddhist Council of Bangladesh.[62] When the Pakistani government announced it would look after the reconstruction of the most important among the hundreds of temples demolished in December 1992, construction companies refused co-operation pleading they had been threatened by Islamic militants not to collaborate with "idolatry". At any rate, the number of Hindu temples in these ex-Hindu territories is decreasing even faster than the percentage of Hindu inhabitants. In Great Britain, more than 20 temples were damaged or burnt down after the demolition of the Babri Masjid, and even in the US and Canada, the past decades have witnessed several Muslim assaults on Hindu temples (e.g. Denver 1984, Toronto 1991).

---

[60]*Statesman*, 24-12-1992. "Forthright" in the case of a secularist is what is called "fanatical" when applied to a Hindu. As for "impartial", the paper fails to mention that on that very occasion, the *Panun Kashmir* spokesman questioned Verghese "impartiality".

[61]A. Maheshwari: *Crescent over Kashmir*, Rupa, Delhi 1993, p.221-227.

[62]Sita Ram Goel et al.: *Hindu Temples: What Happened to Them*, vol.1, appendix to the first edition (Voice of India 1990), ch.7 of the second edition (ibid. 1998).

More importantly, temple destruction is a small matter compared to another development in Kashmir: the ethnic cleansing of the near-total Hindu population, a quarter-million people, from the Kashmir Valley in early 1990. It remains for future students of political and communications science to describe and explain the unbelievable phenomenon of a world press keeping the lid on this information. Rosenthal's own *New York Times* is among the papers which have created the impression, with effective consequences for US foreign policy, that the Kashmir conflict is between hapless Muslims and an ugly Hindu state machinery, a distorted impression which would have been corrected to a fair extent if the paper had faithfully reported the undeniable Islamic persecution of the local Hindu minority.

For India-watchers in academe as much as in the media, it is impossible to comprehend the communal conflict in India, including the Ayodhya affair and the Bombay riots, as long as they keep on closing their eyes for facts (repeat: facts) like the "ethnic cleansing" of Hindus in Kashmir. From the US government, I could still understand why it wilfully ignored an inconvenient case of ethnic cleansing in Kashmir, or why it publicized much-exaggerated figures for the Bosnian "genocide"; after all, it is in the business of conducting politics (i.e. arming Pakistan and Bosnia), not of seeking the truth. But from American journalists and academics, the persistent denial of the forced exodus of the Kashmiri Hindus is inexcusable.

1.2.8. Hindus discriminated against

According to Rosenthal, one propaganda item which stimulates Hindu hatred of Muslims, is that "they are 'pampered' by the central government". The same sentiment, similarly interpreted as the result of false propaganda, is cited by Susan Bayly, and in fact by most critics of the Hindu movement. As a starting-point for evaluating the claim that Hindus are discriminated against,

I would like to quote Susan Bayly's correct initial observation that "it would be wrong to think of the [Ayodhya-related violence] as an outburst of incomprehensible bloodletting".[63] Far from being the irrational behaviour of inherently riot-prone savage natives (the picture you get in some Western and Indian English-language reporting), these riots are the outcome of deliberate strategies and ideological positions.

Unfortunately, both Mr. Rosenthal and Mrs. Bayly are unable to see the hard reasons behind Hindu militancy, because they are caught in the over-all bias of most "secularist" writing on the phenomenon of "fundamentalism", viz. that external (non-doctrinal) factors can account for it. A very common expression of this bias is the reassuring explanation that there are no inherent religious reasons for the recent upsurge in Islamic militancy, and that it is all due to post-colonial frustrations or rising unemployment. In the case of "Hindu fundamentalism", the usual explanations are full of Marxist phraseology about "the urban traders seeking to assert themselves" or "an upper-caste ploy to prevent Backward-casteist mobilization", or other conspiracies of interest groups *masquerading* as religious movements. This approach is an intellectual disorder which one might call "deep thinking": the refusal to look at facts as they present themselves, because of the apriori assumption that what you see is not what you see, that there is something else behind it.

Thus, while any "Hindu fundamentalist" you talk to, will tell you that Hindus feel like second-class citizens in India, Susan Bayly makes no attempt at all to find out the factual basis of this complaint. On the contrary, she makes it impossible for herself to comprehend Hindu activism by assuming beforehand that India guarantees "constitutional even-handedness to citizens of every religious community and ethnic group". This then is the major reason for the

---

[63]Susan Bayly: "History and the fundamentalists: India after the Ayodhya crisis", *Bulletin of the Academy of Arts and Sciences*, April 1993.

general misperception of the Hindu movement in the West: ignorance or denial of the objective factors of the Hindu unrest, one of them being the legal inequality which Hinduism suffers in India.

The Indian Constitution and legislation are a major cause of religious tension precisely because they contain serious discriminations on the basis of religion. Article 30 gives minorities the right to set up and administer their own government-aided educational institutions, whereas Hindus can only have secular schools or expensive private schools. This blatant discrimination exists not only in the cold print of the Constitution, but is also an undeniable fact of life: Hindu organizations like the Arya Samaj and the Ramakrishna Mission have had to go to court to ask recognition as religious minorities in order to gain rights denied to them as Hindu bodies.

Similarly, the management of Hindu temples is almost entirely controlled by the State governments (implying: their funds directed to non-Hindu projects, their priests terribly underpaid, in some cases their upkeep grossly neglected), while churches and mosques are entirely controlled by the respective religious communities.

Another inequality is the existence of separate Civil Codes for the different religious communities. Unlike all secular states, India divides its population in Parsi, Christian, Muslim and Hindu (which for this purpose includes Buddhist and Sikh) communities which each have their own personal laws. To give the classic example: a Muslim can marry four wives, while the others cannot. The fact that rather few Muslims exercise the option of polygamy, while many non-Muslims do have mistresses, is immaterial to the fact of the legal inequality: Muslims can practise polygamy legally, others only illegally. There are effectively cases of Hindus seeking conversion to Islam in order to enjoy the right to polygamy.

The common "secularist" defence that real life shows more equality regarding polygamy than the letter of the unequal laws suggests, is unproven and beside the point. Justifying legal inequality on the plea that it is without object in practice is unacceptable: if equality is hard enough to realize in practice, it should at least be upheld in the ideal construction of the legal system. Imagine someone in the USA proposing a law granting tax-exemption to billionaires "except blacks", with the plea that "there are hardly any black billionaires anyway"; or a tax cut for farmers in Germany "except for Jews", on the plea that "there are no Jewish farmers anyway". Imagine the outcry such an unequal law would raise, and keep in mind that the same type of legal inequality actually exists between Hindus and Muslims in India.

Moreover, the religion-based personal laws are not only different, they have also received different treatment from the legislative and executive powers. While no government would dare to amend the personal law of a minority without the latter's prior consent or initiative, the secular parliament has amended the Hindu Law in the 1950s without seeking the opinion of the Hindu community as such or of the acknowledged religious leadership. Thus, the practice of polygamy and that of polyandry once common in Indo-Tibetan communities has been prohibited by a secular parliament not accountable to the communities affected.

A number of minor inequalities can be enumerated, among the latest being the 1991 law granting a statutory status to the Minorities Commission, which now has to be consulted on matters affecting communal relations but from which Hindus are by definition excluded. The government also patronizes or sets up financial institutions specifically for the minorities. Further, there are inequalities which are not formally based on religion though their obvious purpose is anti-Hindu.

Thus, Art.370 gives a special status to Kashmir, which has

its own separate Constitution, and makes possible the prohibition to non-Kashmiris to own property in Kashmir. Though complex historical factors including the policies of the last Hindu Maharaja of Kashmir help explain Kashmir's exceptional status, today the obvious intention behind the preservation and strengthening of Kashmir's separateness is to guarantee the existing Muslim majority there. This is not only an unsecular concern from which a secular state should abstain, it also forms an inequality between Muslims and other minorities: the northeastern Christian-dominated states and Sikh-majority Panjab are not granted a separate Constitution.

None of the inequalities enumerated exist in any secular state. Those who know these facts and still call India a secular state, are simply dishonest; and those who are not aware of them, are not qualified to write on secularism or on the religio-political situation in India. Those who want to abolish these inequalities, are turning India not into a theocratic but into a genuinely secular state. In that sense, the BJP is right when it calls itself "fully committed to secularism" and when it denounces the other parties as "pseudo-secularists". The only sense in which the BJP is "anti-secular" is that, like the other parties, it has little intention of implementing this programme of secularization, justifiably fearing that the enactment of a Common Civil Code would cause a mullah rebellion with plenty of useless bloodshed.

1.3. PROPAGANDISTIC USE OF COMMUNAL VIOLENCE

When it comes to creating an enemy-image, nothing is as useful as human blood. The targeted hate-object has to be depicted as violent and cruel, the favoured group as bleeding under the blows inflicted by the hated group. In a prolonged conflict, you typically get victims on both sides, but then the trick consists in selective reporting. Thus, numerous Hindus have been killed by Christian separatists in Nagaland and Mizoram, yet the outside world believes that it is the meek

Christians who are threatened and persecuted in India by the ugly fanatical Hindus because all the media coverage has been given to the killing of a few Christians in Orissa. Hindu-Muslim riots are another fruitful field of distortive reporting to foster an enemy-image.

1.3.1. The silent slaughter of Hindus

Way back in 1992, "An Islamic group, Muslim Jihad Force of London, has issued a death threat to the leader of the Bharatiya Janata Party, Mr. L.K. Advani (...) in a letter posted from Oman on December 28".[64] Five years later, the deed had still not been done, but the flame of desire was burning afresh. Members of *al-Ummah* confessed involvement in the bomb attack against a BJP meeting where L.K. Advani was expected.[65] The torch had passed from one group to another, but their goal was the same, as was their motive: Islamic *jihad*, war against the infidels.

On 15 February 1998, bomb attacks against an election meeting of the BJP killed more than 40 people. The perpetrators were apparently enemies of the BJP, while the victims were most certainly BJP members and sympathizers. Yet, a Reuters despatch printed in newspapers around the world pretended not to know against whom the attacks were directed; from its reporting, you might just as well deduce that Hindu nationalists themselves had thrown the bombs.[66] This is the closest it gets: "The bomb attacks are a direct consequence of the electoral campaign. They took place just before L.K. Advani, leader of the Hindu party BJP, was to give an electoral speech."[67] Incidentally, it is not true that the bomb attacks were a "consequence" of the election

[64]"Muslim group threatens to kill Advani", *Economic Times*, 9-1-1993.

[65]"To kill Advani is our aim", *Organiser*, 20-12-1998.

[66]"Geweld luidt Indiase parlementsverkiezingen in" (Dutch: "Violence rings in India's parliamentary elections"), *De Morgen*, 16-2-1998, datelined Reuters, New Delhi.

[67]"Geweld luidt Indiase parlementsverkiezingen in", *De Morgen*, 16-2-1998.

campaign: even in the years before the electoral campaign, at least since the Bombay blasts of 12 March 1993, bomb attacks against Hindu Nationalist targets have been a regular fact of life, though I know of no Western paper or academic publication which has cared to mention the phenomenon.

Actually, we learn from Indian sources that Advani only escaped death because his plane arrived three hours late: "His plane was due to land at Coimbatore at 1:30 p.m. and the public meeting was due to begin at 3 p.m. The series of bombs including the 70 kg car bomb were all fitted with timers due to go off around 4 p.m. and the first blast took place at 3:45 p.m. Advani's plane was two and a half hours late and by the time it landed at Coimbatore the bombs had all exploded. (...) The 70 kg load of gelatin sticks kept in a car in the proximity of Advani's meeting place failed to go off due to a technical error committed by the bomb makers. If only this car bomb had exploded at the time of Advani's meeting the casualties and damage would have been unimaginable."[68]

Perhaps the Reuters reporter did not have all the facts yet when he sent his first report; but what he certainly knew, and conspicuously failed to explicitate, was that the victims were BJP supporters. Not that Reuters has anything in principle against naming a victim, judging from its reporting on other matters in the same article, e.g.: "The BJP pleads for segregation between Hindus and other communities, of which *the Muslims are the main victim*."[69] During this research, I have not come across even a single BJP resolution, manifesto or speech which ever called for Hindu-Muslim "segregation" (quite the opposite), but let that pass; the point is that Reuters has no hesitation in naming a victim of this non-existent BJP policy.

By contrast, in this wave of terrorism against the BJP (a new high in a campaign of anti-BJP terror which has been

---

[68]T.V. Rajeswar: "Islamic militancy in India", *Hindustan Times*, 9-4-1998.

[69]"Geweld luidt Indiase parlementsverkiezingen in", *De Morgen*, 16-2-1998; emphasis added.

striking now and then since March 1993), Reuters leaves its information consumers to guess who the victim was, and whether the BJP was the perpetrator or the target of the violence. Nothing in the 94-line report explicitates that the violence was directed against the BJP, eventhough that was the first and only fact of which we could be certain right away (in most murder mysteries, the killer may remain unknown for a while, but the victim is known right from the start). The policy seems to be, not to concede anything whatsoever to the Hindu movement, not even its martyrs.

Indeed, some people, like the then Congress president Sitaram Kesri, have immediately tried to shift the blame onto the Hindu victims. David Frawley, an American Hindu and Vedic scholar, reports: "The recent Coimbatore bombing that killed a number of BJP workers was likened in the *New York Times* to the Reichstag fire which Hitler staged to gain power. The implication was that the BJP planned the bombing as an election ploy, even sacrificing its own members, and that they are as ruthless as Hitler.[70] That Islamic terrorist groups were directly linked, was ignored. (...) Some of these charges reflect propaganda from Indian sources, like Sitaram Kesri of Congress who cast blame on the BJP for the Coimbatore bombings."[71] Shielding the perpetrators and attacking the

[70]The comparison is completely contrived. That Hitler staged the Reichstag fire was Communist propaganda; the fire was started by the Dutch Communist Marinus van der Lubbe, though Hitler drew a certain profit from the event; but he was already in power and didn't need to "gain power" anymore. While the *New York Times* accuses the BJP of killing its own people for propaganda reasons, neither Van der Lubbe nor Hitler saw the Reichstag, the House of Parliament representing bourgeois democracy, as "his own". (KE)

[71]D. Frawley: "The elections in India and their portrayal in the media", unpublished paper (but available on *www.vedanet.com*), p.5. Frawley adds the typical American reason for choosing the Muslim side in India's religious conflict: "The US government has had a strategy to defend Muslim causes outside the Middle East, while it dominates Islamic countries within the Middle East. This helps prove to Muslim groups that the US is not anti-Islamic. It can be used to distract their attention to other regions in the world so as to diffuse any possible Islamic hatred of America."

victims: along with Hindu Revivalists, the neutral observer must raise the question *why* Hindus are getting such vicious treatment in the world media.

When Muslim atrocities against Hindus are mentioned at all in the media, an attempt is usually made to shift the blame back to the Hindus. Consider *Masala*, a special issue (1995) of *India Nu*, the bimonthly periodical of the Dutch *India-Werkgroep Nederland*, which devotes one chapter to each South-Asian country. The Bangladesh chapter by Jeffrey Eshuis does list facts about the Islamic campaign against Hindus, e.g. in December 1993, "dozens of Hindus were killed and many more wounded. More than 2,000 women were raped. As a consequence, many Hindus fled to India. In the northern Bogra district, where the riots were the most violent, 25% to 30% of the Hindu population is said to have left since 1993. In the Chittagong Hill Tracts (...) autochthonous people (Buddhists, Hindus, Christians and Animists) are forced to convert to Islam and women are forced to marry Muslim Bengali settlers."[72] But in his general introduction, the editor hastens to shift the blame to the Hindus: "One can see Muslim communalism in Bangladesh as a reaction to Hindu fundamentalism in India".[73]

But at least he didn't censor out the facts of atrocities against Hindus. By contrast, the expulsion of the Kashmiri

---

[72]Jeffrey Eshuis: "Fundamentalisme en machtsstrijd in Bangladesh" (Dutch: "Fundamentalism and power struggle in BD"), *Masala*, p.8.

[73]Dick Kooiman: introduction, *Masala*, p.5. In the same issue, Pakistan-watcher Willem Oliemans claims that Pakistan is "not fundamentalist" (p.23), that Pakistani fundamentalists "are but a fringe group" (p.23), though "Islam lies at the basis of Pakistan" (p.24), and that "there is little danger that Pakistan becomes an Islamic state" (p.28)! Just as there is no need for carrying water to the sea, there is no need for a fundamentalist movement which seeks to turn Pakistan into an Islamic state, for *Pakistan already is an Islamic state*, where a Sharia Court can overrule any democratically enacted legislation if it discovers anything un-Islamic in it. The same paper which describes a Hindu movement as "fundamentalist" for allegedly wanting to declare India a "Hindu state", denies the "fundamentalist" character of an established "Islamic state".

Pandits in early 1990 has gone practically unreported outside India. Most experts, including the contributors to *Masala*, somehow pretend to explain "Hindu fundamentalism" without even one reference to the expulsion of the Hindus from Kashmir, the single most important example of the "plight of the Hindus in secular India" cited by Hindu activists in the 1990s.

A Hindutva commentator observes: "Curiously, the world powers and the high-profile human-rights organisations are dubiously silent when any atrocities are perpetrated by the Muslims towards the Hindus and other minorities in Bangladesh."[74] Starting from that observation, it is argued that this neglect is by no means innocent. The Bangladeshi government knows very well that it is heavily dependent on Western aid, and it will go out of its way to eliminate phenomena which give it a bad press internationally. Hence, if the international media were to keep a close watch on the treatment of the minorities in Bangladesh, it would save lives.

Indeed, Prof. Saradindu Mukherji alleges a causal link between the media's non-interest and the effective policies in Pakistan and Bangladesh: "Once the Islamic rulers realised that the Hindus were nobody's concern, they did not waste any time to show the Kafirs their real status."[75] Victim groups tend to be relatively protected by media publicity, and the strict denial of such publicity to the Hindu minorities in Bangladesh and other countries contributes to the continuation of their oppression.

1.3.2. Manipulated riot reporting

The general image of Hindu Revivalism is shaped less by

[74]Raman Bando: "Minorities in Bangladesh", *Organiser*, 16-2-1997. See also V.P. Bhatia: "Thrown to the wolves. Bangladesh — a concentration camp for minorities", *Organiser*, 14-4-1996, and: "The plight of Bangladeshi Hindus: beggared, outraged and levelled to dust both by India and Pakistan", *Organiser*, 21-4-1996.

[75]S. Mukherji: "Harassed Minorities of Bangladesh", *Times of India*, 15-11-1994.

ideological statements in books than by newsworthy events and the way these are reported in the media. Considering that blood is a priceless influencer of people's sympathies, riot reporting is a favourite hunting-ground for aspiring moulders of public opinion. The Indian language press provides examples of wilful distortion in both pro-Hindu and anti-Hindu senses (for the former, gross examples can be cited from the Shiv Sena's Marathi paper *Sâmnâ*, "Confrontation"), but the English-language papers which determine the international impression of India's communal situation have specialized in the anti-Hindu variety, at least in the 1980s and early 90s.

When individual commentators try to shape public opinion, there is often not more to their exercise than a clever use of language. Thus, Asghar Ali Engineer, in his article "Communal fire engulfs Ahmedabad once again"[76], accuses the BJP of having engineered the Ahmedabad riots of 1985, and promises proof: "The opposition parties, particularly the BJP, has played by far the most important role in the continuing violence, specially in its communal form. We will throw more light on this question."[77] After some pages about inter-caste violence, he repeats his allegation: "Whatever the role of the Solanki government and whatever its sins of omissions and commissions, the opposition parties, particularly the BJP, had played no less sinister a role in provoking communal violence. It played this role from behind the scene and very cleverly. This came out in our talk with a number of knowledgeable people in the field as well

---

[76]Asghar Ali Engineer: *Communalism and Communal Violence in India*, Ajanta, Delhi 1989, p.256-284. Ahmedabad provides a case study in Islamic strategy as well as in the nexus of religious strategists and the underworld, vide e.g. Mayank Jain: "Minority becomes majority — majority becomes minority: a first-person report from Ahmedabad", *Organiser*, 15-11-1998, which deals with the tactics used since the 1970s to chase Hindus from targeted areas of the city in order to buy the real estate for a small price and repopulate them with Muslims.

[77]A.A. Engineer: *Communalism and Communal Violence*, p.257.

as with the intelligent observers of the socio-political scene."[78] In the next twenty pages, Engineer quotes many people, no doubt knowledgeable and intelligent, on many aspects of the Ahmedabad riots, but the BJP is not mentioned anywhere. By the end of his paper, without offering a trace of proof, Engineer has probably managed to make many a reader believe that the BJP hand behind the riots is an established fact.

But there are more powerful agencies than mere verbal manipulations to influence the public perception of the division of guilt for communal violence. Since the national and state governments have mostly been controlled by secularist parties, the lead was often given by politicians and their dependents. The Bhagalpur riot of 1989, one of the biggest massacres in India since Partition, provides a case study in manipulation at the source, viz. the politically appointed official enquiry committee. The one-man commission consisting of Justice (retd.) R.N. Prasad was not finding a BJP or otherwise "Hindu communalist" hand behind the riots, so the State Government of Bihar led by Laloo Prasad Yadav expanded the commission to three members. The two new members then duly made the required "discoveries" and brought out another report (of which Justice Prasad dissented in a statement gratefully reproduced in *Organiser*), finding the BJP guilty.[79]

The Bhagalpur carnage figures as a classic proof that India's communal conflict is one between Hindu bullies and Muslim victims, one which India-watchers paint in truly genocidal colours. Thus, Peter Van der Veer, commenting for Flemish radio on the communal situation, said that in the 1989 riots in Bhagalpur, "a small village", the Muslim presence had

---

[78] A.A. Engineer: *Communalism and Communal Violence*, p.262.

[79] That at least is Justice Prasad's testimony: "Bhagalpur riot panel report", reproduced in *Organiser*, 16-7-1995, and: "Chairman's report on Bhagalpur riots: bombs were thrown at Ramshila procession from Muslim high school", *Organiser*, 23-7-1995.

been "annihilated".[80] The Bhagalpur riot took a terrible toll among Muslims, which the fact that the Muslims started the violence in the first place cannot justify; nevertheless, Bhagalpur still has a large Muslim population, and Bangladeshi infiltrators still consider it safe enough to settle there in their thousands. In fact, the migration figures are the best refutation of the "Hindu bully, Muslim victim" myth: as against the constant trickle of Hindu refugees out of Pakistan and Bangladesh, there is no Muslim flight out of India, but on the contrary a massive Muslim influx into India.

Concerning the Jamshedpur riots of 1979, routinely blamed on the RSS by communalism-watchers (e.g. by leading journalist M.J. Akbar)[81] and by secularist politicians, *Statesman* columnist S. Sahay alleges a gross distortion, not in the enquiry committee's report itself, but in the summary given by the Bihar Government and widely quoted in the media: "It can be said without any hesitation that the summary of the Narain Commission's report released by the Bihar government was highly selective, and in that sense tendentious. (...) It wholly ignored the commission's findings on the immediate and surrounding causes, or the role of extremist Muslims who clearly started the riots by throwing stones on the Ramnawami processionists.(...) It needs to be remembered that it is by no means the commission's finding that the RSS, as an organization, had caused the riots. (...) Having persuaded itself that the two communities, Hindus and Muslims, had by no means declared war against each other, that only some extremist elements had gone berserk, and that there was no preparation by either community to cause riots, the commission was confronted with the task of

[80]BRTN (now VRT) Radio 1, 12-12-1992.

[81]M.J. Akbar: *Riot after Riot*, p.24 ff. Akbar claims as his source "a local politician", apparently a Congressman like M.J. Akbar himself (who was elected from Kishanganj in 1989 against Syed Shahabuddin, but defeated by Shahabuddin in 1991), with Congress then (1979) in the opposition against the RSS-supported Janata Party.

blaming some organization for the riots and it chose the RSS."[82]

Both the BJP and the RSS countered the Bihar Government's version, but their account never got the kind of publicity which was given to the official one.[83] Though the commission had an unmistakable pro-Muslim bias, and therefore tried to twist aggression into self-defence, it could not help registering the well-known fact that, after all was said and done, it was Muslims who started the violence. According to Sahay: "One notices a good deal of sympathy, undoubtedly well-deserved, for the Muslims because in most cases it is they who were the victims. The commission has concluded that 'acting under panic, for which there was sufficient cause, the Muslim minority had planned to the extent of preparing themselves against an attack by the Hindu communalists. The anti-socials among them turned this preparation into aggressive action.'"

The "panic" was caused by the fact that the procession came near the Muslim neighbourhood and halted there, not by any actual Hindu violence. "However, panic alone cannot explain why the Ramnawami procession had to be stoned. The commission is to be faulted for not making a clear distinction between decent, law-abiding Muslims and the Muslim hooligans, and for not going deeply into their strength and activities, especially when the death of an anti-social, Anwar, in an encounter with the police, had caused resentment among the extremist section. This is the more so because the commission's clear finding is that it is the Muslims who started the riot by throwing stones on the procession."[84] True, the Muslim rioters suffered serious

[82]S. Sahay: "A close look. Jamshedpur riots report", *Statesman*, 24-9-1981.

[83]A rebuttal by the BJP of the Government's version was prepared by Ram Jethmalani and Sikander Bakht: *Jamshedpur Riots: the Truth Unmasked.* The RSS published its leader Balasaheb Deoras' *Speech in Jamshedpur* (1-4-1979), to prove that it did not contain "inflammatory" statements which had "provoked" the Muslims and "sparked" the riots, as had been alleged.

[84]S. Sahay: "A close look. Jamshedpur riots report", *Statesman*, 24-9-1981.

losses, but that doesn't exculpate them, or at least some of them, from the over-all guilt for the outbreak of the riot. Yet, the image which remained in the collective consciousness once the details were forgotten, was of a pitiable Muslim minority pushed around by an overbearing Hindu majority.

1.3.3. Who starts the riots?

Till today, Hindu-Muslim riots in India, Pakistan or Bangladesh are almost always started by Muslims. In the case of Pakistan and Bangladesh this is entirely obvious: no Hindu would dare to offend the Muslim majority there. On the street, they are simply no match for the Islamic fanatics, and the police or the judiciary cannot be counted on to protect them or do them justice.

If you don't believe Hindu sources, consider the US State Department report on human rights in Pakistan. It found that "Hindus complain of continued kidnappings and forced conversions of young women, desecration of Hindu shrines and temples, disruption of prayer services and the burning of Hindu texts as well as the torture of detained Hindus.(...) in Sargodha, on February 25, 1992, a magistrate sentenced four Ahmedias to 8 years rigorous imprisonment and a fine of about $ 32 for having built an Ahmedia house of worship in their own land. Anti-Ahmedi plaintiffs had charged that the 'non-Muslim' place of worship injured their religious feelings.(...) Many Christians fear the forced marriage of Christian women to Muslims."[85] Constant fear and walking on eggs not to offend the Muslims in any imaginable way have become a way of life for the non-Muslims in Islamic states.

In the case of India, the Muslim initiative is obvious in many incidents if you take the trouble of getting the details of how a riot started (sometimes reported in the press, often wilfully withheld). As even the fundamentalist Maulana Wahiduddin Khan admits, giving the examples of Aligarh riots of October 1978 and Moradabad riots of August 1980,

[85]"US report indicts Pak for rights abuses", *Times of India*, 15-2-1993.

Muslims "drunk on the liquor of emotionalism" had started them: "The first started because a Muslim wrestler Ansar Ahmed and his men killed a Hindu wrestler Suresh Bhure who had defeated him in a *dangal*. The second started because of the Muslims' attack on a marriage party of Balmikis when they refused to stop the playing of band, etc., near a mosque."[86]

However, in the biggest riots, the Muslim initiative is often obscured by the fact that the final victim toll typically shows more Muslims than Hindus killed. Before such figures, lazy-minded observers immediately conclude that it must be a case of a brutal majority oppressing a poor hapless minority. Yet, the very fact that such riots have become big two-way battles in the first place proves that these are definitely not confrontations between a fearful minority and an overbearing majority.

Where that is the case, as in Pakistan and Bangladesh, you never see the fearful minority fighting back. All that the Hindus there can do, is to make themselves as small and invisible as possible, pay hefty bribes for some safety, acquiesce in the abduction of a daughter for forcible marriage to a Muslim, agree to sell their real estate for a ridiculous price in exchange for their lives, and move to the last remaining zones of concentrated Hindu habitation, or better still, to India.[87] So, in Pakistan and Bangladesh, you some-

---

[86]Summary of a speech by Wahidduddin in V.P. Bhatia: "Muslims start the riots", *Organiser*, 7-3-1993. According to Bhatia, the Maulana was "dubbed 'RSS maulana' not long ago by the likes of Syed Shahabuddin for bluntly telling Muslims that almost every riot in free India was started by them". *Dangal*: wrestling tournament, arena.

[87]The problem of the abduction of non-Muslim women was highlighted in a US State Department report on human rights in Pakistan, which found (as reported in "US report indicts Pak for rights abuses", *Times of India*, 15-2-1993) that "Hindus complain of continued kidnappings and forced conversions of young women, desecration of Hindu shrines and temples, disruption of prayer services and the burning of Hindu texts as well as the torture of detained Hindus.(...) Many Christians fear the forced marriage of Christian women to Muslims."

times get large-scale hunting-parties with the Muslims as hunters and the Hindus as prey, you also get petty terrorizing all the time, and equally unilateral; but you never get confrontations in which Muslims and Hindus fight each other.

In India, by contrast, Muslims have often put up a brave fight. In many cases, they had stockpiled arms beforehand. And sometimes they think they can get away with unprovoked attacks. Even in cases where it is widely assumed that it was Hindus who attacked first, the Muslims did consider fighting a realistic option, which provides a significant contrast with the position of the minorities in Pakistan.

Consider this neutral report on the start of the Meerut riots, still regularly cited in pro-Muslim sources as proof of Hindu-cum-police terrorization of the poor hapless Muslim minority: "The city of Meerut in Uttar Pradesh, which saw bloody Hindu-Muslim riots in 1982, was the scene of communal violence again in May [1988]. An attempt by police to arrest a Muslim for the murder of a Hindu in a land dispute exploded into ten days of mayhem that left over 150, mostly Muslims, dead."[88] So, it started with a Muslim killing a Hindu and a Muslim mob seeking confrontation with the police by trying to prevent it from pursuing a murder investigation; and it ended with "mostly Muslims" dead. In spite of their ultimate victimization, it was the Muslims themselves who were responsible for the outbreak of the riot. From a count of corpses, you cannot deduce which party was guilty of the riot which produced the corpses.

1.3.4. Riots, terrorism and the death toll statistics

A very influential instance of manipulative collusion between governments, journalists and also academics, is the death toll statistics. These indicate that in the past fifty years, at least twice as many Muslims have been killed in communal violence as compared with Hindus. That picture changes

[88] *Encyclopedia Britannica*, Yearbook 1988, entry "Hinduism".

completely when we also consider the far higher figures for Pakistan and Bangladesh, but even for India, the over-all picture is not rendered accurately by these figures. Whether Muslims are indeed more numerous in the death toll of Indian religious violence, depends on which cases of violence are selected.

Thus, during the Rushdie affair, both in Mumbai and in Karachi, Muslims were killed by the police when they threatened to attack British and American consulates; the circumstances of the killings were exactly the same, yet in the Mumbai case, they have been included in the tally of atrocities on Muslims proving how unsafe Muslims are in "Hindu India". For a more consequential example, Christophe Jaffrelot's figure for the deaths in communal violence in 1993 significantly includes the 557 victims of the Mumbai riots of January 1993, mostly Muslims, but not the hundreds of victims of the bomb blasts in March, mostly Hindus, nor the several dozen victims of the subsequent bomb attacks against RSS-BJP personnel.[89] That way, it is of course easy to minimize Hindu victimhood and present India's Muslims as a persecuted hapless minority.

Now, a case could be made that terrorist bomb attacks simply fall in a different category of violence than street riots. Alright, but in that case, why doesn't Jaffrelot, along with most other authors on communal violence, give a statistic of terrorist violence alongside that of street riots? I will not speculate on motives, but the outcome of publishing that other statistic would be this. It would make crystal-clear that the immense majority of terrorism victims in India have been Hindus, and that the perpetrators have in most cases been Muslims. This would be in line with international trends, where the last quarter of the 20th century witnessed incidents

---

[89]Christophe Jaffrelot: *The Hindu Nationalist Movement*, p.552.

of Islamic terrorism in numerous countries, efforts at denial notwithstanding.[90]

Second in rank among the perpetrators would be the Communists, though their murders of Hindus should probably not be classed under communal violence, for the victims are not killed because of their religion, but because of their social status, e.g. landlords. Needless to say, terror has always been an intimate companion of Communism. In the two decades preceding the October Revolution, leftist terrorist attacks killed or seriously wounded 17,000 people in Russia, e.g. a famous bank robbery in Tbilisi 1907 to finance the Communist Party left dozens of bystanders dead or mutilated.[91] In recent decades, Communist countries like the German "Democratic" Republic have supplied know-how, training and weapons to terror groups in every continent, while Cuba gave asylum to hijackers. In India, terror and intimidation against Hindu nationalists and other political rivals are routinely practised, not just by outlaw militias like the People's War Group but also by the establishment CPM.[92]

---

[90]An explicit effort at denial is Bruce Lawrence: *Shattering the Myth: Islam beyond Violence*, Princeton University Press, 1998. Note the prestigious publisher: no Islam-critical book would get that red-carpet welcome. The US supports Islam on many fronts, disregarding the anti-American slogans in Islamic demonstrations, partly to humour Islamic regimes and counterbalance their displeasure at American support for Israel, and partly because the Islamic world is the perfect market: large and in many places very rich, but not a dynamic competitor, hence complementary with the US. Hindu India, by contrast, is limited as a market but is a dynamic competitor, and it doesn't have to be humoured concerning the Middle East. So don't expect a Princeton edition of the present book, which merely takes issue with the myth of Hindu fascism, whereas Lawrence can afford to deny the worldwide fact of Islamic terrorism.

[91]Ann Geifman: *Thou Shalt Kill: Revolutionary Terrorism in Russia 1894-1917*, Princeton University Press 1993.

[92]E.g.: H.V. Seshadri: "RSS deplores Marxist violence" (on murders of Hindu nationalists by CPM workers in Kerala), *Organiser*, 20-10-1996; Mohammed Javed: "CPI-M/Trinamul clashes claim 20 lives", *Rediff on Net*, 28-1-2000; "8 bombs seized from CPM office in Midnapore", *Times of India*, 27-5-2000.

Next in line are the Christian separatists. In their case, it is very hard to get an accurate estimate, also because the death toll should be divided into fellow Northeastern tribals refusing to convert (such as the Riang tribe, collectively expelled from Mizoram in the late 1990s); Hindus stationed there as Government servants, and killed either as representatives of the state or as Hindus; Hindu refugees from Bangladesh; Army personnel regardless of religion; and others.[93] The phenomenon of Christian separatist violence is seriously underreported, and I have talked with journalistic "experts" on India who weren't even aware of its existence.

At the time of writing, we can mention a fourth factor of anti-Hindu terror in the past tense (but we must touch wood, for the deeper ideological causes have not been neutralized): the Khalistani movement. In the years 1980-93, the Sikh separatists have practised indiscriminate terror as well as actions specifically targeting Hindus or Hindu nationalists. Unlike the Hindu-Muslim conflict, the so-called Hindu-Sikh conflict saw no street riots, it only had a terrorist dimension. The only time when the Khalistani terrorists managed to provoke street violence from non-combatants was when they murdered Prime Minister Indira Gandhi, leader of the secularist Congress Party: whereas Hindutva activists took as many Sikhs as possible to safety (with Vajpayee in person saving a Sikh taxi driver), Congress secularists showed their true colours by killing several thousands of Sikhs. It really was a family quarrel among secularists: the pro-Union secularists of Congress versus the Khalistani separatists who equally fervently claimed to be secularists because they undeniably were enemies (in effect, mass killers) of Hindutva communalists.

By contrast, ever since the murder of the Mahatma, Hindus seem to have lost all taste for terrorism. In the spring of 2000, a series of bomb attacks on churches, sometimes

---

[93]Vide e.g. Vijay Chand Dugar: "Mizo extremists on the rampage. Non-Christian inhabitants flee the state", *Organiser*, 5-4-1998.

accompanied by Hindutva pamphlets, seemed to set a new pattern, proving that Hindus are no better than Muslims. These bomb attacks fed the Church campaign against "Hindu fascism" some new and eagerly publicized evidence. But on 17 July the truth came out: members of a Islamic group, *Dindar Anjuman* (founded in 1924 under the Nizam's patronage in order to convert synthesis-happy Hindus with claims of an underlying unity of all religions), were arrested and found to be in possession of both explosives and home-made Hindutva pamphlets, and they confessed to having committed the bomb attacks in order to provoke Hindu-Christian hostility (after having similarly desecrated Ambedkar statues to foment clashes between Dalits and the RSS).[94] Expectedly, the Christian information channels which had earlier trumpeted the Hindu aggression were slow in communicating the correction.[95]

As usual, the Hindus had been falsely accused of stooping to the same behaviour level as that of their enemies. But as it turned out, they were innocent. Since this might be reckoned as a virtue, all opinion-makers in India and abroad have (so to speak) conspired to keep this out of view.

1.3.5. Starting the Bombay riots

For a case study in manipulation of riot information by the media, let us look more closely into one extremely

---

[94]On 4 August 2000 (23h30 GMT), BBC-World broadcast a debate between Christian spokesman John Dayal and BJP spokesman J.P. Mathur. The latter was a very ineffective debater, a typical RSS gerontocrat who hasn't noticed that the new media require new skills. He failed to win anyone's confidence with his claim that "a conspiracy" with a "foreign" hand behind it had engineered the bomb blasts and put the blame on the Hindus. I don't know about India, but I can assure you that every Western viewer despises such explanations. And yet, Mathur had a point: the head of the *Dindar Anjuman*, Zia-ul-Hassan, turned out to be a Pakistani.

[95]After checking some European Christian papers which had earlier carried stories of the bomb blasts prominently, I had to turn to *Organiser*, 30-7-2000, for the details of the true story, esp. S.V. Seshagiri Rao: "Blasts in churches: propaganda and the truth", and N.S. Rajaram: "Anjuman Deendar cult".

consequential case of media bias in the reporting of an event: the Mumbai riots of December-January 1992-93. These have been described in the world media as "pogroms" committed by well-prepared and well-armed Hindu death squads against poor defenceless Muslims.[96] The term has been used systematically in practically all foreign media, even by people regularly employed in *Hindu* publications and broadcasts.[97] Yet, a close reading of the initial reporting on these riots (as opposed to the later references in comments) suggests that both in December 1992, in the aftermath of the Ayodhya demolition, and in January 1993, the initiative had been taken by Muslims.

To decide whether a riot is a "pogrom", one cannot get around the question: who started? When inconvenient, people always dismiss this question as puerile, only good for boys fighting in the playground and complaining to the intervening teacher that "it's he who started, not me!" But in fact, the adult world too tends to treat this question as crucial in the ethical evaluation of acts of violence. Thus, the bombing of Dresden in early 1945 is always justified with the

---

[96]E.g. by Abraham Rosenthal in his column on the Bombay riots in the *New York Times*, reproduced in the *Times of India*, 5-3-1993. Notice the tactic of the "circular argument of authority": first Indian media like the *Times of India* feed foreign correspondents their version of the facts, which then gets reproduced in prestigious foreign media, only to be recopied from there in the same Indian media, with the implied message: "Look how the enlightened West supports our viewpoint." Likewise, the diagnosis "anti-Muslim pogrom" was given by Jim Masselos: "The Bombay riots of January 1993: the politics of urban conflagration", *South Asia*, vol.17, 1994, p.86.

[97]The Hindu-born Surinamian-Dutch journalist Anil Ramdas, who regularly hosts talks for the Hindu programme on Dutch TV, published an edited transcript of his TV talk with Ashis Nandy and Arvind Das (NOS 3, 3-5-1993) in *De Groene Amsterdammer*; though both secularist guests took a rather balanced and anti-dramatic view of India's communal situation, the title given to the text consisted of a single word: "Pogroms", based on Das's statement: "It was *almost as if* an organized pogrom". Another regular collaborator of the Dutch Hindu programme, Peter van der Veer, likewise summarizes the Bombay riots as "pogroms": *Religious Nationalism*, University of California Press, Berkeley 1994, p.7.

argument that the Germans could easily have avoided it by not *starting* the war. So, the question may be asked in all seriousness: did Hindus or did Muslims start the riots?

In the case of the post-Demolition riots of December 1992, the Muslim initiative is universally conceded, and is already very probable if we consider what happened outside India: in England, Bangladesh and Pakistan, there have been unilateral large-scale attacks on Hindus and Hindu property (e.g. 22 Hindu temples damaged or destroyed in England, and 3,600 in Bangladesh)[98], the violence was 100% Muslim, with only Hindus, Hindu temples and Hindu property as victims (apart from a few Pakistani Muslims shot down by the Pakistani police, not by Hindus).[99] In Kenya, the Emirates and other countries, threats against Hindus were made by Muslim spokesmen, not the other way around. Are we to believe that Indian Muslims were less enraged than their foreign brethren by the violation of Islam's God-given right to occupy Hindu sacred sites? Of course not: the situation in Mumbai was no different from that in Karachi or Dhaka.

After the riots started, the police did its duty, and tried to stop the rioters. For some reason, the Indian police always

98"3,600 temples destroyed in Bangladesh", *Times of India*, 19-3-1993. According to Sudhangshu Shekhar Haldar, MP for the Awami League opposition, "40,000 Hindu homes were burnt and 10,000 minority businesses looted in the communal disturbances which left 15 people dead". The credibility of at least one of these figures is undermined by the strange disproportionality between the number of houses and businesses attacked and the number of people killed.

99Two exceptions to the rule deserve mention: in Ayodhya itself, Hindutva militants attacked some Muslim houses, killing at least one Muslim who, moreover, had come out in *support* of the projected temple; and in Surat, no refutation has been forthcoming for the allegation that the rape of Muslim women was a unilateral act of aggression by Hindus, perpetrated immediately after the first news of the Demolition had come in; though Sudhir Chandra ("Of communal consciousness and communal violence: impressions from post-riot Surat", *South Asia*, vol.XVII, 1994, p.55) relates that "the Surat riots are perceived as a Hindu reaction to Muslim action even by scholars who are not Hindu communalists — one of them is a Christian priest".

uses bullets instead of teargas, so that a substantial number of rioters were killed. Since the rioters were Muslims, this means that the police killed Muslims. Immediately, the secularists were out to accuse the police of being "communal". When I asked a Mumbai policeman about this, he said: "What should we do? Should we shoot even-handedly at both the attackers and the people whom they attack?" Considering the vogue of quota, this sounds like a promising application of the principle of communal equity: equal bullets for aggressors and victims (and similarly: equal punishment for rapists and their victims, etc.). As a reaction, secularist authorities gave the police instructions to be nicer to Muslim rioters.

A journalist reports: "The city has witnessed a carnage. That it has been one of Muslims by a partisan police force is becoming increasingly clear."[100] A secularist comments: "Why should we be surprised then that more than 90 per cent of those who have died in the violence in Bombay have been Muslims and that the vast majority of them died from police bullets. During the short lull between the last round of riots in Bombay and this one I visited some of the city's trouble spots and did not come across a single victim who had not died from a police bullet."[101] A Muslim is quoted to the same effect: "On a side-street in Bharatnagar, a slum colony near Bandra, Mrs. Naseem Khan, a schoolteacher sobs tearfully: 'They are firing at innocent people. This is not a Hindu-Muslim riot, but a police-Muslim riot."[102] A Muslim member of the Mumbai Municipal Corporation, Ahmad B. Zakaria, is quoted as seeing "the violence as beginning due to communal provocations but escalating because of the city police. 'No one can deny that there were anti-social Muslim elements who were out to create trouble.'"[103] But then, the

[100]*Sunday Observer*, 13-12-1992.

[101]Tavleen Singh: "The rift is widening", *Indian Express*, 17-1-1993.

[102]"Bombay police under fire for shooting to kill", *Times of India*, 11-12-1992.

[103]*Sunday Observer*, 13-12-1992.

initiative to riot was generally justified as an understandable reaction to the "provocation" which the demolition of the Babri Masjid had been.[104]

The focus in the comments was not on the Muslim initiative to riot, but on the police brutality in suppressing the rioters (and it must be admitted that police in India are inordinately quick to use gunfire rather than teargas).[105] Secularist politicians and journalists accused the police of being "communal". *Time* magazine quotes a Human Rights watcher with approval: "The riots were presented to the world as communal clashes between Hindus and Muslims. In fact they were Muslims vs. the police, who seemed to have a Muslims-only trajectory for their bullets."[106] At any rate, the police were not forgiven for their tough handling of the riots, and were subject to a certain demoralization. It is important to keep this in mind when trying to understand the riots of January 1993, when Muslim rioters targeted the police while the Shiv Sena claimed its hand was forced by police inaction.

1.3.6. Manipulated riot reporting: Mumbai, January 1993

I had heard many Hindus complain about the unfair reporting, but when I asked them to document their complaint, I found that nobody even cared to collect newspaper clippings (it is part of the RSS culture to go by rumours rather than verified hard information). The one exception was Shrikant Talageri, who took the trouble to go to the library and look up the relevant press reports; to prove his point, he sent me an essay, *The Bombay Riots* (so far not published anywhere), about the media coverage of these

[104]This explanation is noted, possibly with a smirk, in Salman Rushdie: *The Moor's Last Sigh*.

[105]E.g.: "Bombay police under fire for shooting to kill", *Times of India*, 11-12-1992.

[106]Jefferson Penberthy: "Might vs. Rights", *Time*, 18-1-1993, quoting Ravi Nair, executive director of the South Asia Human Rights Documentation Centre, Delhi.

riots, quoting from the *Times of India* accounts and adding some interesting observations. The present section and the next (1.3.5-7) summarize his argument, except for adding some quotations from other journalistic accounts to put it into perspective.

The Mumbai riots of January 1993, which killed perhaps 600 people, had been started by the Muslim side, as admitted by prominent Muslim spokesmen, e.g. Iqbal Masud, a Marxist Muslim, observes: "There was an attack by Muslims in Bombay police station. On January 7 and 8, 1993, there were some attacks by Muslims on Hindus in Bombay, Grant Road, etc."[107] Likewise, an editorial sums up: "It is a fact that a small group of anti-social elements among the Muslims ignited the fuse this time round by setting fire to some shops owned by the Hindus".[108]

Even the otherwise secularist film industry has confirmed this version of the facts in Mani Ratnam's 1994 film *Bombay*. The Bombay film industry is the most powerful anti-Hindu propaganda medium, because unlike the secularist press, it actually reaches the common Hindu people. In film after film, it vilifies Brahmins, propagates Urdu and mocks proper Hindi, puts padres and mullahs in saviour roles, and glorifies marriages between Hindu girls and their Muslim suitors. Yet, the truth about the origin of the riots was so undeniable to everyone in the greater perimeter of the city that even the film makers could not twist it too far. Muslim audiences were angry at Mani Ratnam's film, not just for showing a Muslim girl falling in love with a Hindu (the Muslim philosophy about this, firmly established in the Sharia, is that "our girls are ours, yours are up for grabs"), but also for not confirming them in

[107]Iqbal Masud: "The best PM money can buy", *Pioneer*, 23-2-1996. Nonetheless, Masud does confirm the Muslims in their victim role: "But they were nothing in proportion to the genocide visited on Muslims from January to March 1993. For this not only the Shiv Sena but the Congress under Mr. Sharad Pawar were responsible."

[108]Editorial, *Observer of Business and Politics*, 12-1-1993.

the victim role which they had appropriated in connection with the Bombay riots. Mani Ratnam "had a miraculous escape when a bomb was hurled at his residence in Madras".[109] Both he and his wife were injured.[110] Local authorities banned the film under Islamicist pressure or threats.

So, the RSS version is not too far off the mainstream perception (which does not by itself prove it right, of course): "The worst riots took place in 1993 in the wake of the disputed structure's demolition. And just note how Mumbai Muslims behaved. First, about 100 Muslims (...) burned down Rakmanibai chawl (a Hindu-occupied building) in Jogeshwari suburb of Mumbai. Seven innocent Hindus, mostly women and children, were burnt alive. On the very same day, two Hindu dock workers were killed at Pydhoni area in a Muslim-dominated district of Masjid Bunder area. In the evening, Muslims of Mohammedally area attacked an old Boiwada police building (...) All the three attacks by Muslims were reported in 'secular' papers like *Indian Express* and *The Times of India*. Naturally, Hindus became upset and aggressive. I agree, the retaliation by Hindus was bad (...) But again, who started the riots?"[111]

Yet, the outside world has never heard this account of the January riots because the decisive news channels, first of all the *Times of India*, have chosen to black out all reference to the Muslim initiative. Its reporting during the first three days gives what Mumbai resident Shrikant Talageri considers the true story, though only to the reader who knows Mumbai well: the areas mentioned where "people" and policemen were attacked, were all Muslim-dominated areas.[112] Following Press Council rules, the paper did not mention which community was on the attack and which one on the

---

[109] *The Hindu*, international edition, 5-8-1995.

[110] *De Standaard*, 11-7-1991.

[111] Bharat Ramani: "Distorted presentation of history by Pak media", *Organiser*, 9-2-1997.

[112] Mumbai edition of *Times of India*, issues of 7 to 9-1-1993.

defensive, until three days later, when the Shiv Sena started its retaliation. From that point onwards, the first three days, when Muslims were on the attack (in the inflated rhetoric of communalism reporting, it could have been called a "pogrom" of Hindus by Muslims) were kept out of view, but the details of subsequent Shiv Sena-led Hindu violence against Muslims were reported in full. Also, the death toll of the first three days was not sufficiently spectacular for international media attention, so the foreign correspondents started relaying the version of the Indian media to their own readers from 9 January onwards.

The riots started on 6 January, as reported in the Mumbai edition of the *Times of India* of 7-1-1993: "3 killed, 40 hurt in city clashes". Under those headlines, the following news was reported: "Three persons died and 40 were injured as fresh violence broke out in several communally sensitive localities of the city late last night. The worst affected were Pydhonie, Nagpada, Dongri and pockets of Ibrahim Rahimatullah Road in South Bombay and Dharavi and Mahim in north-central Bombay (...) The injured included three policement (...) For the first time in recent days, curfew had to be imposed at 7 p.m. at Dharavi instead of the usual 10 p.m., as mobsters went on rampage, ransacking carts and pelting stones and bottles."

The next day, the *Times of India* (8-1-1993) had more news: "The trouble reportedly began at around 7 p.m. yesterday, when rumours spread throughout central Bombay that a place of worship was being demolished in the suburbs. The first incident reported to the police was that of a taxi-driver who was stabbed to death in Pydhonie at around 7:45 p.m. Thereafter, several reports of violence were received from Pydhonie, Dongri, Nagpada, and V.P. Road, the police commissioner said." Talageri claims that all the areas mentioned are predominantly or exclusively Muslim.

On page 3 of the same issue, we see a set of photographs with the following caption: "A man who was stabbed, flees from a mob near J.J. Hospital junction on Thursday (above) to fall near a police van." According to Talageri, the story behind the photographs is this: "On 7 January, mobs of Muslims in the Muslim areas named above fanned the streets and caught passers-by on the busy roads. Those suspected to be Hindus were made to remove their pants, and if they were found to be uncircumcised, they were stabbed to death. The police were under strict instructions from the state government *not* to shoot at Muslim mobs. The main area of this activity was in the Muslim heartland in south Mumbai (Bhendi Bazar, Mohd. Ali Road, and Ibrahim Rahimatullah Road upto the above-mentioned J.J. Hospital near Nagpada). The said photographs depict this: in the first, a motley crowd is manhandling, examining and stabbing the man; in the second photograph, the same man, with his pants dropped down his legs, is falling beside a police van nearby, with some policemen quietly watching the whole scene."[113]

On 9-1-1993, the *Times of India* carried the front-page headline "Police chief escapes mob fury, 36 more killed in city", and reported: "Thirty-six people were killed in various incidents of violence across the city today taking the total death toll to 55. Unconfirmed reports put the toll at 75.(...) Most horrific of all the incidents of violence sweeping the city was the 5 a.m. attack on Radhabai Chawl in Jogeshwari. Four people, including three women, were locked in their homes in this colony perched atop a hillock off the Western express highway, and burnt to death by a frenzied mob.(...) Though curfew in the predominantly Muslim areas of Central Bombay had been lifted from 12:30 p.m. to 2 p.m. to permit *namaz*, residents of the area stayed on the streets and engaged the police and others in fire and petrol bomb attacks." The "four people burnt to death" were Hindus, the "frenzied mob" was Muslim; in conformity with existing Press Council rules, the *Times of India* obscured this fact, but the

[113]Talageri: "The Bombay riots" (unpublished paper), December 1996.

informed reader could deduce it from the details given.

So, in Talageri's reading, for three whole days the *Times of India* faithfully reported that it was Muslims on the rampage, though without saying it in so many words. Describing any subsequent violence against Muslims as a "pogrom" would be an insult to the memory of the historical victims of authentic pogroms: Jews in Czarist Russia who were *attacked without provocation*.

From 9 January onwards, the Hindus, who had been demoralized by the blaring media propaganda since the demolition, "gathered their wits together" (Talageri's term) and went on a rampage in their turn, in retaliation against Muslim violence which had already killed a dozen Hindus, quite unlike the unilateral "pogroms" of European history. The term *pogrom* has a precise established meaning, and the Shiv Sena action starting on 9 January 1993, no matter how regrettable otherwise, does not satisfy its definition. Distorting the established meaning of an intensely charged term like *pogrom* for the obvious purpose of maximum stigmatization is a practice which has no place in objective scholarly (or even deontologically sound journalistic) discourse, and disqualifies sources or authors as biased and unreliable.

1.3.7. Judging the Shiv Sena's counter-offensive

To establish the secularist media's double standards, Shrikant Talageri draws attention to the editorial comments in the *Times of India*. On 9-1-1993, the editorial is titled: "Anarchy in Bombay". At that time, the Muslims had been on the rampage for three days, while the Hindus had not yet retaliated in prominent measure. Yet the editorial totally fails to pinpoint or even mention the Muslim rioting; it is rather as if some impersonal violence has somehow befallen the city. Far from showing concern about the Muslim aggression, the esteemed paper indulges in some general platitudes and gives the following advice to the authorities: "The administration will also have to contain the provocative *maha-aartis* which have been organised throughout the city." So, to stop Muslim violence, it is the Hindus who have to be curtailed.

In this version, the "anarchy" which is troubling Bombay is caused by the public prayer meetings which the Hindus organized in reaction to the Muslim Friday prayer sessions which for quite some time already tended to spill over into the streets and disrupt the traffic. If the *Times of India* meant to say that Muslim violence is the normal result of these "provocative" *maha-aarti*s, then this would imply a back-handed compliment to the Hindus: instead of responding to the provocative Muslim show of power (street-blocking *namaz*) with violence, they controlled themselves and responded with a mere counter-display; the Muslims, by contrast, escalated the confrontation from the symbolic level to that of physical violence. Before the esteemed paper could face the facts of the ongoing violence, it chose to wait until after the Hindus had started retaliating in kind, and then it suddenly started to give communal labels to the forces deemed responsible. On 12-1-1993, after three days of Shiv Sena vengeance killing several hundred, the editorial's title is: "No will to govern". It reads: "There is a marked difference between the riots that took place in Bombay after December 6 and those a month later. While the first were sparked off by Muslims who were incensed by the destruction of the Babri Masjid, these appear to be the handiwork of organisations whose diabolical object is to terrorise Muslims by destroying their property. The scene of the riots has shifted from the slums and chawls to the more prosperous central areas, which happen to be where some Hindu militant bodies have their strongholds. There is a method in the madness that has descended on the city and there has virtually been a pogrom declared against Muslims. Only homes, shops and cars belonging to them have been singled out for attack, which bears the stamp of a systematic vendetta. Muslim militants have also been arming themselves in some instances, but the harsh reality is that this community has borne by far the biggest brunt of the riots."

That seems to be an accurate description of the situation on 11 January 1993, the *sixth* day of the riots; but it cleverly disregards the causes of this development. But we now have it from a quotable secularist source that at least the preceding December riots were "sparked off by Muslims". Less elevating are the excuses which are immediately added: if you are "incensed by the destruction of the Babri Masjid", no word of condemnantion for your rioting crosses the lips or the computer keyboard of our secularist editor. So, if a single building with mosque architecture is destroyed, this justifies nationwide (and beyond) Muslim violence, but if almost every remaining Hindu temple in Pakistan, Bangladesh and Kashmir is destroyed, this does not justify even the "provocative *maha-aarti*s".

Other papers admitted that the January riots had been started by the Muslim side even when trying to apportion a maximum part of the blame to the Shiv Sena, e.g.: "It is a fact that a small group of anti-social elements among the Muslims ignited the fuse this time round by setting fire to some shops owned by the Hindus; but it would appear that the criminals on the other side of the communal divide were waiting in the wings and have exploited this alibi to wreak vengeance with fury on innocent Muslims."[114]

On 15-1-1993, the *Times of India* headline read: "Shiv Sena admits to role in Bombay riots". The article, signed by Rajdeep Sardesai, says: "The riots in the city have been systematically engineered from Saturday onwards by the Shiv Sena in tandem with anti-social elements." Follows a long story purporting to reveal "the plan decided upon in the shakhas" (i.e. the local "branches" of the Shiv Sena). The paper's tactic is clear: from now on, the Bombay riots have

[114]Editorial in *Observer of Business and Politics*, 12-1-1993.

started on Saturday, 9 January, and whatever happened on the three previous days will be blacked out from all further references to the "Bombay pogrom". In its first-hand reporting, the *Times of India* itself had described murderous assaults by Muslims without mentioning any comparable Hindu assaults or even retaliation for three days, — a Muslim *pogrom* of Hindus, in the full sense of the term (though sadly for them, they fared like all those aggressors who underestimated their victims, and met their Stalingrad). But in spite of this well-attested Muslim aggression, now suddenly the January riots become "the handiwork of organizations whose diabolical object is to terrorize Muslims" and "a pogrom declared against Muslims".

Rajdeep Sardesai was mistaken if he thought he made any revelation to his Mumbai readers by writing that the "Shiv Sena admits to role in Bombay riots". True, in the later controversy over the Srikrishna Commission's report on the Bombay riots, an admittedly biased report written under instructions of the then ruling Congress Party and shamelessly whitewashing Muslim violence all while putting the Hindu side in the dock, the Shiv Sena tried to wimp out by ordering the discontinuation of the Srikrishna inquest and by denying its allegations.[115] But in 1993 the Shiv Sena was still quite outspoken about its role, so that the defensive word "admit" is entirely misplaced. The Sena's explanation was that when the police failed to discharge its duty, it merely gave the lead to the citizens of Mumbai in defending themselves. However, even when the Shiv Sena repeatedly and proudly

[115]The one-person Srikrishna Commission was mandated by the Congressite government of Maharashtra to investigate the causes of the Bombay riots. It was dismissed by the subsequent SS-BJP state government (vide Muzaffar Hussain: "The sack of the Shrikrishna Commission", *Organiser*, 7 and 14-4-1996), but reinstalled at the behest of the 13-day BJP-led central government of June 1996, in a typical bid by the BJP to prove its secularism. The report produced by Justice Srikrishna only proved the suspicions of bias which had led the state government to dismiss it.

asserted its role in fighting for the Hindus in the riots, it has never admitted to having *started* the riots.

But why fuss about the details? The *Times of India* has succeeded in its Goebbelsian design: the world has never heard about the Muslim initiative in the Bombay riots, and even well-meaning people like Abe Rosenthal think of them as a "pogrom", inflicted without provocation by mean and hateful Hindus on an unsuspecting Muslim minority.

1.3.8. The impersonal mode in riot reporting

The then *Times of India* editor, Dileep Padgaonkar, offers what amounts to a textbook illustration of biased anti-Hindu reporting in his book on the riots of January 1993, *When Bombay Burned*. When Hindus are killed, he and his sub-editors stick to the Press Council rules, so that the violence is very impersonal and the perpetrators remain unidentified: "The knives flashed out again in Dongri, Pydhonie and Nagpada" and "in Dharavi (...) mobs killed four people" (Muslim-majority areas where Hindus were killed); but when a Muslim is the victim, we are left in no doubt about his communal identity: "24-year-old *Mohammed Shaukat Ali* (...) nursing a broken arm, relived his ordeal."[116] Likewise, "thousands of *mathadi* workers gathered to participate in a condolence meeting for two of their brethren murdered the night before", but the Hindu identity of these victims can only be deduced from subsequent hints of "communal" overtones in the speeches made at that condolence meeting. By contrast, a Muslim victim is readily identified as Muslim: "a Muslim *mathadi* worker had been killed in broad daylight".[117]

The use of the impersonal mode is the typical style whenever a Muslim initiative in communal violence is described. Thus, M.J. Akbar, after relating the itinerary of a

---

[116]Clarence Fernandez & Naresh Fernandes: "A City at War with Itself", in D. Padgaonkar: *When Bombay Burned*, UBSPD, Delhi 1994, p.45; emphasis added.

[117]C. Fernandez & N. Fernandes: "A City at War with Itself", in D. Padgaonkar: *When Bombay Burned*, p.42-43. *Mathâdi* = "porter".

Hindu procession on that fateful 11 April 1979 in Jamshedpur as far as the immediate vicinity of a mosque, describes the moment when the palpable tension was transformed into actual violence: "At 11:40 a.m. the inevitable happened. A stone was thrown. A bomb exploded. The rest was murder."[118] Nobody actually did it, it just "happened", the bomb simply "exploded" somehow. Considering the claims by other respected intellectuals about "the role of extremist Muslims who clearly started the riots by throwing stones on the Ramnawami processionists"[119], and considering Akbar's explicit objective of putting the blame on the RSS (that "most dangerous clandestine force, determined to provoke violence")[120], it is quite likely that his vague formulation was his way of keeping the RSS under a cloud of suspicion without having to make a precise allegation which others might refute.

Likewise, Iqbal Masud exonerates the Muslims for the Islamic bomb attacks on 12 March 1993 with a typical invocation of unnamed "criminals", all while deploring the bomb blasts' side-effect of terminating the Mumbai Muslims' victim role: "The March 12, 1993 bomb blast hit back by mafiosi was politicisation of criminals. The moral foreground was taken over by the BJP after the 'hit back'."[121] But if the Muslims were the victims in January, how can the bomb blasts in March be a "hit back" unless they were perpetrated by Muslims, even if qualified as "mafiosi"?

Consider also *Time* magazine's reporting on the Mumbai riots of December 1992, about which nobody denies the Muslim initiative: "In nationwide communal riots that erupted after Hindu fanatics destroyed the Babri mosque in the town of Ayodhya, 1,200 people were killed".[122] The Hindu attack

---

[118]M.J. Akbar: *Riot after Riot*, p.28. On p.27, Akbar himself mentions that Muslims as well as Hindus in the area concerned were "prepared for battle".

[119]S. Sahay: "A close look. Jamshedpur riots report", *Statesman*, 24-9-1981; see also above, Ch.7.1.4.

[120]M.J. Akbar: *Riot after Riot*, p.25.

[121]Iqbal Masud: "The best PM money can buy", *Pioneer*, 23-2-1996.

on the Babri mosque was committed by "Hindu" fanatics, of course; but the Muslim retaliation was not the handiwork of "Muslim" rioters, it merely "erupted". No doubt similar tricks are also used in a pro-Hindu and anti-Muslim sense, but in the media which matter internationally (including *Penguin*, which publishes M.J. Akbar's books, and *Time*), I have so far only seen it done in the opposite sense.

This kind of distorted reporting is powerful not by its cleverness (it is transparent and predictable), but by the key positions in the media where it is deployed: most international India reporting consists in copying the *Times of India* (this is not a secret, the reader can verify it from the sources explicitly quoted in Western newspaper articles about India). However, it is by no means innocent. The bombs killing about 400 people, nearly all of them Hindus, in Mumbai on 12 March 1993 (exploded in public buildings including the Stock Exchange on Friday around noon, when devout Muslims are in the mosque) were by all accounts a Muslim retaliation for the January "pogrom". But that "pogrom" was a media invention which replaced the actual facts of bilateral violence ultimately started by Muslims. With this atrocity propaganda, the media provoked the Muslims into a "retaliation" which was all too real.

None of this goes to justify the Shiv Sena excesses, but then neither can the Shiv Sena excesses justify journalistic manipulations, especially not when these have equally lethal consequences.[123]

1.3.9. Hindu militancy and the common Hindu

---

[122]Jefferson Penberthy: "Might vs. Rights", *Time*, 18-1-1993. In this article itself, the Muslim initiative can indirectly be inferred from the claim, cited with approval, that the clashes were not "between Hindus and Muslims" but "Muslims vs. the police".

[123]It is a strange phenomenon that whenever I mention the actual proportion of Hindu and Muslim deaths in religious violence in South Asia, there is always someone ready to warn against using this estimate to "justify" Hindu violence; I have so far never read or heard this reaction when others *falsely* create the impression that it is mostly the Muslims who suffer.

Another aspect of the media disinformation about the Bombay riots is the claim that both Hindus and Muslims have been disillusioned with the Shiv Sena because of its role in the riots. In reality, the Shiv Sena leadership role in stopping the Muslim pogrom of the Hindus endeared the party to the majority of the Hindus in the whole of Maharashtra. I have met non-political people who said that they were grateful to the Shiv Sena for protecting the Hindus against the Muslim attacks, for, as a nurse put it to me, "who knows what would have happened to us without the Sena?"

Using opinion-polls and interviews with the carefully selected "man in the street", some newspapers may have created a different impression, but the real expression of the people's opinion is still through the ballot box. In the Maharashtra Assembly elections following the riots (1995), the SS-BJP alliance won a solid majority in the state, and won 30 out of the 34 seats in the city. Three seats in Muslim areas were won by the National Front / Left Front, and the only more or less Hindu area where the BJP-SS alliance lost, was where it had put up a defector candidate (who had contested earlier elections on Congress and NF-LF tickets). Though the SS was once hostile to all non-Maharashtrians, particularly South Indians and Gujaratis, the SS-BJP alliance won in all other Hindu-majority districts, including the Gujarati and South-Indian areas.[124] In the 1996 Lok Sabha elections, the SS-BJP alliance once more did very well. (In 1999, when the Sena's "merits" during the riots were forgotten, disgust with Shiv Sena corruption caught up with the coalition and sent it back to the opposition benches.)

If the Mumbai riots had really been a Hindu pogrom of poor hapless Muslims, these election results would stamp not just the SS but the whole (or at least a decisive electoral

---

[124]The SS victory among Gujarati *Bania*s, Mahatma Gandhi's community, is particularly significant, considering the irritation which Bal Thackeray has often caused among them with his frequent crude remarks about the Mahatma.

majority) of the Hindu community in Mumbai as inhuman. That is the impact of biased riot reporting and of the stigmatization of Hindu organizations as "fascist": it affects Hindu society as a whole. Among overseas Hindu communities, such as the Surinam Hindus in Holland, I notice how intimidated they are by the systematic association of Hinduism with "communalism". Thus, in the Dutch Muslim TV programme, you see combative discussions about controversial issues, including polemic against other religions (e.g. in a documentary about one Dutchman's conversion to Islam, the classical arguments against Christianity were raked up), but in the Hindu programme, all controversial topics are strictly avoided. But when you talk privately to them, their sympathies are with those who stand up for Hindu assertiveness, because they know which Indian community is within its rights and which one is the aggressor.

In this case, the Shiv Sena action was indeed supported by Hindus of all stripes including non-Hindutva elements. Thus, "a Congress corporator was shot dead [by the police] 'while she led an armed mob against a Muslim slum'."[125] A young man, Ashwin Shah, "a Youth Congress leader in Dadar", describes how he set the whole stock of a Muslim-owned bookshop on fire: "All this trouble was started by Muslims. They killed two mathadi workers on Mohamedali Road, the public was quiet. They killed Hindus in Behrampada and Malad. Still we were quiet. But the public was provoked by what happened in Jogeshwari (the burning of a hut in which four people were roasted alive setting off the fresh bouts of riots in January). It is not the Shiv Sena or the BJP that caused all the damage. It was the Hindu public."[126] It was the common Hindu who felt indignated at the Muslim attacks, and he needed no Hindutva

[125]Swapan Dasgupta: "Message of Bombay", *Sunday*, 24-1-1993, citing the *Hindustan Times*.

[126]Maria Abraham: "Running riot", *The Week*, 14-2-1993.

indoctrination to recognize the aggressor and opt for self-defence.

During the Partition riots, in East Panjab and in Calcutta, Hindus took revenge on Muslims for the annihilation of the Hindu presence in West Panjab and parts of East Bengal. Among these killers were people belonging to Hindutva organizations (e.g. Madanlal Pahwa, an accomplice in the Mahatma Gandhi murder), surely, but also secular socialists like Ram Manohar Lohia, who killed Muslims and distributed weapons to the Hindus in Calcutta, as became known when many of these weapons were surrendered to Mahatma Gandhi after his epic Calcutta fast. The Hindu-Muslim conflict is a profound reality of Indian society, not an artificial creation of RSS propaganda, and it can trigger events without needing any specific RSS initiative.

To sum up, the Shiv Sena got a lot of bad press when it reacted in strength against a series of Muslim attacks on Hindus in early January 1993. When the police, still sulking after criticism of its "anti-Muslim attitude" in an earlier round of communal violence (December 1992), refused to act against the Muslim rioters, Bal Thackeray's activists took the law into their own hands. Even years later, no SS spokesman is apologetic about this operation: they see it as a necessary intervention in a Muslim attempt to take over of the city with street terror. To keep this violent confrontation in perspective, it should be recalled that it remained an exceptional event: even after some 300 Hindus were killed in Muslim bomb attacks against Hindu or predominantly Hindu targets, including a failed one against the Sena headquarters, the Sena did not react, and preferred to avoid further escalation. Tough guys don't exaggerate.

Compared to the violence to which Hindus in Pakistan and Bangladesh have been subjected, and which is entirely one-sided, the violence record of the Shiv Sena, and even that of all Indian Hindu and Muslim communalists combined, is peanuts.[127] That is why level-headed Hindus keep a sense of proportion in judging the Sena's counter-offensive of 9 January 1993: this is not what they want, it should not be repeated, but in the circumstances, it was an understandable excess, of an altogether different character and a lower magnitude of horror than the endless series of unprovoked Islamic attacks on Hindus.

1.3.10. What's so radical about the RSS ?

Hindu radicals see nothing radical about the BJP and the RSS, vide e.g. Arvind Ghosh's pamphlets *What is Wrong with the BJP?* (Houston 1996), and *It is Good for the BJP if L.K. Advani Retires Now* (Houston 1995), triggered by Advani's presiding over the wedding of his niece to a Muslim, on which occasion she converted to Islam. In particular, they laugh at secularist claims that the RSS is a dangerous militia. At the height of the Ayodhya campaign, when the RSS seemed to be setting the agenda, a radical Hindu group in Great Britain published a pamphlet with the unambiguous title: *RSS is Paper Tiger*.[128] Arguing that the RSS did not fire a single bullet to prevent the Partition or the post-Partition slaughter of Hindus, the authors warn:

"Ignoring all the past, the Hindus have once again pinned their hopes on the RSS though RSS has *not* got a single gun, not even kitchen knives, to defend themselves against the Muslims and the Mujahideen when the next onslaught against the Hindus comes. (...) Seen in this light, RSS achievements to date are dismal though to all the mice a rat looks like a giant. A sighted idiot is an object of great wonder to the blind! We live in the world of tigers and wolves — those who kept us in bondage for 1,000 years, and those who snatched our five provinces without firing a pistol shot in 1947 when RSS was

---

[127]About more recent rounds of violence against the minorities in Bangladesh, see Taslima Nasreen's famous documentary novel *Lajja* (1994), or Bangladesh Hindu Buddhist Christian Unity Council: *Communal Discrimination in Bangladesh: Facts and Documents*, Dhaka 1993.

[128]The Institute of Hindu Ideology (PB 42, Wellingborough NN8 3HL, Great Britain): *RSS, a Paper Tiger*, 1991.

only armed with sticks and twigs and could act *nowhere* to despatch traitor *Nehru* to the next world or the treacherous Muslims to their 'homeland' (Pakistan)."

In the present as in the past, the RSS fails to live up to its image: "It is failing us now (it is *no* factor in the reckoning of J & K Liberation Front in the Valley) and it will fail us tomorrow. (...) 'Where is the RSS?', ask the defenceless Hindu girls in Baramula, Srinagar and Anantnag. They do not realize that RSS is only a paper tiger to impress the Hindus living in the dingy basement — at best a bluffing roadroller that becomes feather-light in Kashmir due to *fear*."

The martial display of the RSS is contrasted with its failure to upset the secularist establishment, and this contrast is likened to the Sikh soldiers in the British colonial army parading their martial attire but actually serving the enemy cause like donkeys in a treadmill: "Despite all this incompetence, RSS has acquired a very powerful image among the downtrodden Hindus. This is like the grand image of symbol-bearing Sikhs during the British Raj. They 'shot' bitterly at any symbol-less Sikh, while doing a 'deep salaam' to every clean-shaven British official wearing a hat!"[129]

So, that is how radical Hindus (who, to my knowledge, have never pointed a gun at a real enemy either) evaluate the RSS performance in physical confrontations. For all its intemperate language, this pamphlet may well have a serious core of truth to it. RSS spokesman Narmohan Doshi has a point when he claims: "The Sangh believes in non-violence".[130] The Indian establishment insists that the RSS is "the world's largest private militia", but against this tall claim, Gérard Heuzé stays closer to the facts when he points out that

---

[129]In the British policy to separate the Sikhs from Hindu society, the Khalsa emblems (most notably turban and beard) were falsely identified as a minimum requirement for recognition as a Sikh. Sikh soldiers in the British army took these misconceptions home and started terrorizing the Sikh community into conformity with this puerile innovation.

[130]Narmohan Doshi: "The Sangh believes in non-violence", *Organiser*, 5-4-1998.

"the way in which the RSS was overwhelmed by a thousand determined youngsters on 6 December 1992 is telling. The sect is worthless in street combat (...) Its manifestations remind us more of the boy-scouts than of mass politics".[131] Again, fascism should be made of sterner stuff.

1.3.11. BJP aggression and victimhood in the balance

"None of the present BJP front-benchers is likely to outlast the BJP revolution; their fate will resemble that of the initiators of the French Revolution who stormed the Bastille in 1789: their followers will take care of them as they did at Ayodhya [on] 6 December 1992."[132] That is the prediction by a leading Congressite about what would happen if ever the BJP comes to power: in his view, the mild-mannered BJP leaders are merely the vanguard, preparing the field for a hard-line group of Hindu "fundamentalists" and "fascists". Judging from the first years of the BJP in power, this prediction now stands as a howling failure.

Having talked with hundreds of BJP and RSS activists, from Balasaheb Deoras, Rajendra Singh, Ashok Singhal, L.K. Advani and Murli Manohar Joshi down to the ordinary Sangh or BJP workers, and including notorious fire-breathers like Vinay Katiyar and Sadhvi Ritambhara, I have yet to meet these hidden hardliners. To be sure, I have heard second-rank BJP politicians and Bajrang Dal activists justify the use of violence, — but when I inquired a bit deeper, they clarified that they meant self-defence, after other means had been exhausted, etc., just the universal consensus, in India noteworthy only because of the contrast with Mahatma Gandhi's extreme and unrealistic pacifism. For rabble-rousers, they were rather timid when compared to the casteist party leaders (the type of Mulayam Singh Yadav)[133]

[131]Gérard Heuzé: *Où va l'Inde Moderne?*, p.122.

[132]Mani Shankar Aiyar, "True Visage", *Sunday*, 10 December 1995.

who are quite open in their advocacy of intimidation and violence; or to the Communist parties, which have retained the violent overthrow of liberal democracy as their stated long-term project, and which for practice apply muscle methods against their Hindutva rivals.

It is already a breakthrough that a Congressite openly admits the distance between his hypothetical second-level fanatics and the front-rank BJP politicians. That is an improvement upon the picture we get in the international media, with L.K. Advani as a "hate-mongering demagogue" and A.B. Vajpayee as "a wolf in sheep's clothing". About the national BJP leadership, any impression of extremism ought to be removed by a close look at their actual record, including their off-the-record statements.

During the Ayodhya campaign, its leader L.K. Advani was never caught in the act of making even a single anti-Muslim remark. Of course the assumption that Muslims had destroyed Hindu temples in the past was underlying the whole issue, but that assumption is historically fully accurate. The talk of "revenge" on the Muslims which his enemies and the press have attributed to him, is fictional. Advani's position was that Muslims ought to make a gesture to make a clean break with this chapter (which is not distant history, given what Muslim fanatics have done to Hindu temples in Kashmir and Bangladesh), and that the restoration of a single one of the thousands of temples forcibly replaced with mosques would suffice. The VHP asked for three places out of thousands, Advani cut that number down to one, — the one in

[133]Mulayam Singh Yadav, who cultivates the Muslim vote bank, has been a hate figure for Hindu nationalists ever since he had the police open fire on the *Kar Sevaks* in Ayodhya in 1990. Nonetheless, he has repeatedly made headlines with political decisions which agreed with or substantially helped the Hindu nationalist position, e.g. in 1999 he torpedoed the Congress attempt to form an alternative Central Government under Mrs. Sonia Gandhi, at least partly because he too rejected the idea of having a foreigner as Prime Minister.

Ayodhya which was already back in use as a Hindu temple since 1949.[134]

But what about Advani's bloody *rathyâtrâ* (car procession) from Somnath to Ayodhya in October 1990? Very simple: it is not true at all that the Rath Yatra was a bloody affair. While in the same period, there was a lot of rioting in several parts of the country (particularly Hyderabad, Karnataka and Uttar Pradesh), killing about 600 people in total, there were no riots at all along the Rath Yatra trail. Well, there was one: upper-caste students pelted stones at Advani because he had disappointed them by not supporting their agitation against the caste-based reservations which V.P. Singh was promoting. Even then, no one was killed or seriously wounded.

It is a measure of the quality of the Indian English-language media that they have managed to turn an entirely peaceful procession, an island of orderliness in a riot-torn country, into a proverbially bloody event ("Advani's blood yatra"). And it was quite a sight how the pressmen in their editorials blamed Advani for communal riots of which the actual, non-Advani-related causes were given on a different page of the same paper. Whether Advani with his *rathyâtrâ* was at 500 miles distance from a riot (as with the riot in Gonda, U.P.), or under arrest, or back home after the high tide of the Ayodhya agitation, every riot in India in the second half of 1990 was blamed on him.

Thus, concerning the Hyderabad riots, the *Statesman*

---

[134]We are foregoing consideration of the more fundamental question as to which is more fanatical: to demand back the sacred places which are those of your own religion, dedicated to your own gods (Shiva, Rama and Krishna), or to wilfully remain sitting on someone else's sacred sites, knowing fully well that they were forcibly taken by your own predeccessors, and knowing fully well that you yourself would not allow anyone to touch your own sacred sites. Obviously, a case could be made that the problem does not lie in the Hindu claim to a Hindu sacred site (Advani's campaign), but in the Muslim claim to a Hindu sacred site; just as in a fight between a house owner and an illegal squatter, the problem is not that the owner claims back his own property.

faithfully reported their Muslim origin (a paroled murder convict called Mohammed killed a policeman, arms caches found in Muslim houses, Muslims keeping up the offensive all through the conflagration), but then on the editorial page it forgot all about its own story and put the riot down to "a spark from Ayodhya", for "it is not clear yet what caused the eruption in Hyderabad. Nor is it worthwhile any longer to look for specific reasons since a focal point already exists: [the BJP's] cynical vote-catching policies relating to the disputed shrines in Ayodhya."[135] Well, even in that communally charged period, the BJP was not a tenth as pugnacious as is always claimed.

The truth is that the BJP is eagerly trying to be nice to everyone (except armed separatists, and even they are politely invited for talks by Prime Minister Vajpayee, whom columnist Varsha Bhosle nicknames "the Mahatma" and suspects of hoping to win the Nobel Peace Prize). The BJP badly wants to be friends with everyone who counts as respectable. Instead of radicalism, the record of its manifestoes, resolutions, interventions in parliament, and public statements, shows a goody-goody approach to all the forces which are animated by a declared and unyielding hatred of Hinduism and of the BJP itself.

These enemy forces don't reciprocate the BJP's niceties. The slow growth of the RSS and BJP in Bihar and West Bengal is due in large measure to the violent intimidation of Hindutva manifestations, and there has never been any Hindutva retaliation in kind. About 400 BJP-RSS workers have been killed by Sikh terrorists in the years around 1990, and there has not been any retaliation either. Fact is also that ever since the Ayodhya demolition, there has been a steady series of bomb attacks on RSS/BJP targets (e.g. killing a dozen people in the RSS office in Madras) and murders of BJP office-bearers: "Bombay BJP chief shot dead"[136]; "BJP activist killed,

---

[135] "Spark from Ayodhya", *The Statesman*, 11-12-1990, discussed earlier in K. Elst: *Ayodhya and After*, Voice of India, Delhi 1991, p.158-160.

violence continues in Tamil Nadu"[137]; "ISI targets South again. Blasts at Munnani and RSS offices linked"[138]; "BJP MLA shot dead in Karnataka"[139], etc. Even the devotional music magnate Gulshan Kumar, "owing to his pro-Hindutva activities, professional and personal", became and eyesore for religious fanatics who killed him in August 1997.[140]

While there is no doubt about the communal identity of the killers, there has been no retaliation by the Hindutva forces. Playwright Safdar Hashmi, who was anti-Congress but even more anti-Hindutva, was killed not by BJP men but by Congress agents. Much fuss has been made of threats against *Jansatta* editor Prabhas Joshi after his criticism of Hindutva.[141] But people who waste breath on verbal threats are not killers, and Joshi escaped the fate of Hashmi and of those dozens of dissident writers in the Muslim world who have been murdered in the 1990s.

Or consider the case of Pu La Deshpande, who was awarded the Marathi literature prize *Maharashtra Bhushan* by the SS-BJP government in 1996. Mumbai VHP president Ashok Chowgule relates what happened: "In his acceptance speech, apart from the usual comments, Pu La made an extremely disparaging remark about the parties in power. He said that while they have promised Shivshahi (rule by the principles of Chhatrapati Shivaji Maharaj) they actually practise thokshahi (rule by muscle power)." To which Bal Thackeray himself expressed his "high respects for the

---

[136]About the murder of Ramdas Nayak, *Indian Express*, 26-8-1994. With reference to earlier murders, e.g. of Prem Kumar Sharma, MLA for the BJP from Mumbai, the paper admits in its editorial comment ("Bombay's bullet culture") that "there are indications that prominent BJP leaders are being specially targeted by terrorists who have large quantities of sophisticated weapons at their disposal".

[137]*Indian Express*, 17-4-1995.

[138]*Organiser*, 30-4-1995.

[139]*Indian Express*, 12-4-1996.

[140]"Gulshan Kumar as promotor of Bhakti music", *Organiser*, 31-8-1997.

[141]Kuldeep Kumar: "Threats, hate mail for Jansatta editor", *Pioneer*, 17-1-1993.

literary contribution of Pu La" but also his disapproval of the remark, rather misplaced in an acceptance speech.

The remarkable thing is that: "In his writings, Pu La has said that he is afraid of taking a stand against the Government. This was much before the Shiv Sena-BJP Government came into power. One does wonder how come he has suddenly mustered the courage to make this allegedly bold statement of his. The conclusion that one arrives at is that in the previous cases, he would have to bear not only verbal 'abuse' but something more. It may well be that he would have been deprived of government patronage — this is something that has happened to others. Or, that he would have been subjected to physical attacks. Yet, the progressives have labelled the present government as fascist, and the previous governments as democratic."[142]

The best proof that the BJP is not fascist, is that people call it fascist and go on calling it fascist, even when its has cadres numbering millions, even when it is in power in the key state of Maharashtra, even when it is in power at the Centre. A fascist government wouldn't let them get away with all this insulting name-calling. By Indian standards, the Hindu nationalist rank and file is not more violent than that of other parties, and probably less so.

1.3.12. Apocalyptic expectations

Like many Western observers, Gérard Heuzé has at one point developed a crisis view of India: "Within the India federation, Bosnias, Lebanons and Palestines are profiling themselves. It is therefore urgent to investigate the aggravation of tensions and the qualitative transformations of violence in the homeland of non-violence. How can one fail to notice that cataclysmic breakthroughs, at the same time resembling and opposing the perspectives of the Iranian revolution, are in preparation after the repeated shocks

[142]Ashok Chowgule: "Of Pu La and progressives", *Indian Express*, 22-1-1997.

which the immense federation is undergoing?"[143]

Many people inside and outside India take the same view: India is on a collision course with itself. Thus, the assistant editor of a militantly secularist paper warns: "Hindu India will have to cope with Muslim India that is likely to emerge very politicized from the Ayodhya crisis and its aftermath. And it would be no ordinary politicization either. According to Max Weber, in times of conflict, Islamic ideology inevitably becomes the focus of political socialization. This can only polarize the country on communal lines (...) This could generate subnationalism of the largest minority group and may culminate in a protracted low-intensity civil war. Gradual internationalization of the Muslim cause and transnational linkages of Muslim response are also not improbable."[144]

Another outspoken secularist comments ominously on a riot, mention of which was "buried in the tenth paragraph of one of those routine riot stories that attempt, in the interest of communal harmony, to tell you nothing". The new element in the riot was that an automatic weapon had been used against policemen. This is the lesson she extracted from it: "Despite the usual attempt to conceal the identity of the rioters, it should be clear to anyone that they were Muslims and that, despite the attempts to play down the event, the arrival of the first AK-47s in a communal riot marks the beginning of what could turn into a full-scale civil war. A civil war that the Indian state appears to be completely unequipped to deal with. Those who think this is an exaggeration need to sit down and analyze what happened in Kashmir and Panjab where a few hundred youths with AK-47s have managed to hold entire states to ransom. Imagine then the situation if every mosque in every Muslim *mohalla* were to consider Kalashnikovs necesary for self-defence? Muslims with AK-47s will

---

[143]Gérard Heuzé: *Où va l'Inde moderne?*, introduction.

[144]Sunil Adam: "The Silent Hindu Majority Has Much to Answer for", *Pioneer*, 23-12-1992. The newspaper has changed hands as well as its tone in recent years.

automatically lead to Hindus with AK-47s and this will begin a cycle of death and destruction (...)."[145]

To put these warnings into perspective, we have to keep in mind that all three of them were written shortly after the riots which followed the demolition of the Babri Masjid; at the time of writing, things seem more peaceful. Remark that the two Indian secularists just quoted foresaw a Muslim initiative in sparking the expected conflagration. And with reason, for Muslim leaders were not afraid to openly threaten violence, e.g.: "Babri Masjid Action Committee convenor Zafaryab Jeelani on Sunday warned the Centre that if minorities were denied natural justice over Babri mosque, it might lead to a Kashmir-like situation in the entire northern India."[146] Likewise, a Muslim columnist writes: "The Muslim minorities all over the world have either engaged the non-Muslim majority in an armed conflict, like the Intifada in the occupied territories, or they have assumed extreme postures, like the Muslims of Cyprus and Sinkiang. Fortunately, the Indian Muslim (with the exception of the Kashmiris) is still non-violent. But no one can say what will happen if the 150-million-strong community is pushed to the wall by Right-wing extremists. Non-Muslims may not be aware of an extremely disturbing development that has been slowly taking place in the Muslim community after the demolition of the Babri mosque. The call for retaliation at various Muslim gatherings are increasingly being heard."[147]

Without imputing a personal responsibility to these spokesmen, it is fair to remember their warnings when one

[145]Tavleen Singh: "The rift is widening", *Indian Express*, 17-1-1993.

[146]"BMAC warns of J&K-like situation", *Observer of Business and Politics*, 4-1-1993.

[147]Syed Zubair Ahmed: "The lesson of Mecca for Indian Muslims", *Times of India*, 19-1-1993. By "the lesson of Mecca" is meant the Prophet's biding his time while being in a marginal position in Mecca, as opposed to his self-confident accession to power in Medina. As for the figure of "150 million Indian Muslims" (ca. 17% of the total population then): Muslim leaders claim that the census systematically underestimates the number of Muslims in India, at that time less than 120 million.

reads about a "bomb attack in Ayodhya railway station prevented when on Ram Navami a railway worker alerted the police to a suitcase standing there abandoned; it turned out to contain 8 kg of explosives, timed to go off when two trains packed with pilgrims were to arrive".[148] Or when on 7-1-1993, a bomb exploded on the Kashi Vishvanath Express near Moradabad, killing a handful of passengers.[149] Have you heard of any similar bomb attacks by Hindus in Pakistan in retaliation for the destruction of Hindu temples in December 1992, or for any of the numerous other acts of violence by Pakistani Muslims against the hapless Hindu minority?

One reason why Muslim leaders and agitators think they can get away with street violence and terrorist attacks is that their community as a whole is not made to pay for it. The demolition of a single silly Babri Masjid was enough to unleash a wave of violence against Hindus in Pakistan, Bangladesh and Great Britain. But when the Pakistani invaders mutilated captive Indian soldiers and tortured them to death in Kargil in 1999, not one Muslim in India was molested. From at least 1993 till the time of my writing, Hindus have collectively kept their cool in the face of endlessly repeated Islamic acts of terror against Hindus in Jammu and Kashmir and elsewhere in India. If you need proof that the morality instilled by Hinduism is superior to that of Islam, there you have it.

Of course, a time may come when Islamic strategists set their sights on more ambitious goals, when they feel they can handle a huge pan-Indian conflagration. At that point, they may deliberately provoke Hindu retaliations against Muslims in order to forge a combative Muslim unity based on hatred for

---

[148]Quoted from *The Hindu*, 29-3-1999, in "Bomaanslag Ayodhya verijdeld", *India Nu*, mei 1999, p.23.

[149]"Bomb blast in train: heroics save the day", *Economic Times*, 9-1-1993. This train was connected with the Ayodhya dispute in that it is named after another disputed site, the Kashi Vishvanath in Varanasi, on which Aurangzeb imposed a mosque, and which is also reclaimed by the VHP.

the Hindus and profiting from the victim role. And conversely, Hindus may at last be provoked into behaving like Pakistani Muslims. This would mean a terrible slaughter which is better avoided, no matter who the victims are; a further stain on the good name of the Hindus, who will at any rate get the blame; and a blow to Hindu self-esteem (the murder of a single Mahatma threw them on the defensive for decades). We should think ahead and prepare for this kind of escalation, in the sense of preventing it.

1.3.13. How to end the riots?

One reason why communal rioters can turn petty quarrels into huge conflagrations, is that they are not stopped in time. In his Indian travel diary for 1928-31, Mircea Eliade, the later pioneer of comparative religion, testified about the riots in the Muslim-majority city of Dhaka: "In Dhaka, Muslims have started riots with the complicity of the police. They attacked the houses of the Hindus, raped the women and slaughtered all those who resisted. They burned down whole neighbourhoods under the eyes of the policemen. These only intervened when a Hindu grabbed a weapon to defend himself. In that case, they entered the house, seized the weapons and arrested the men. The Muslims were armed; they on their part did have that right. All attempts by Congress to bring them to peace have failed."[150]

It is a painful thing to say, but the most successful short-term method to cool down Islamic hotheads has been their defeat at the hands of the police or Hindu militant groups. In the colonial period, a string of Muslim militant movements from the Faraizis to the Khaksars raised their menacing heads in succession, staking their claim to Islamic heaven with acts of terror against Hindus. Sweet talk by Congress leaders and other Hindus made no impression on them, but as soon as British armed might came down on them, their taste for *jihad*

---

[150]Mircea Eliade: *Journal des Indes*, L'Herne, Paris 1992, p.128.

and martyrdom dwindled fast. A few hangings were usually sufficient to chase them off the streets. The Razakars were a terror to the Hindus of Hyderabad, but when Sardar Patel sent his troops in, they disintegrated in no time.

It is routinely claimed that the demolition of the Babri Masjid was an abysmal failure and a matter of deepest shame for pluralistic democratic India; but the fact is that it put an end to a decade of escalating Hindu-Muslim bloodshed. December 1992 (in Mumbai lasting until mid-January 1993) saw a final outburst of communal violence, and then India came to its senses and has been peaceful since. The decisive factor definitely was the tremendous loss of face which the destruction of the Babri Masjid inflicted on the Islamicist leadership. The Muslim masses were suddenly forced to question the wisdom of their fanatical leaders, and to put the business of living before the Islamic cause again. Dozens of major riots which would have taken place had the Babri Masjid continued its intentionally offensive existence, were prevented. This way, thousands of lives were saved in exchange for Babar's monument of victory over infidelism, an undisputably profitable bargain.

Of course, one should not be content with having quenched the fire. It will come back unless measures are taken to change the communalist mentality inculcated into devout Muslims by the Quran and the precedents set by the Prophet. The Indian Muslims have to liberate themselves from the Islamic message of hatred. For a start, the Hindus might take the lead in finding out the true doctrines of Islam, as opposed to the "true, tolerant" Islam which they have invented to soothe themselves. That will help them to distinguish between the Muslims, who are people like everyone else, and Islam, a deluded but combative doctrine which conditions even good people into hating their neighbours and joining attacks on them.

But the familiar lists of hate-mongering verses from the Quran and actual atrocities on unbelievers from Muslim history are not enough to create the proper perspective on

Islam.[151] The intolerance and self-righteousness of Islam are themselves only a by-product of the real problem of Islam: it is but a deluded belief system which could not convince more than a small band of cultists. Even today, with a higher level of scientific education available to the masses than ever before, it remains possible for every self-styled prophet to gather a group of followers around himself and his deluded doctrine; but beyond that, a wall of skepticism blocks the further growth of the cult, wall which can only be broken with military or economic superior force. In the Quran and the Hadis, the injunctions to violence grow in number and intensity in inverse proportion with Mohammed's diminishing hope of winning the skeptical Pagans and Jews over by doctrinal persuasion.

Mohammed's doctrine failed to convince because its distinctive central dogma, that of Mohammed's prophethood, was so obviously untrue. Imagine one of your friends telling you: "I am hearing God's voice; from now on, you have to obey what this voice is saying through me." Of course the Meccans were skeptical, which is why in the Quran, Mohammed is instructed no less than 11 times to disregard the taunts of his countrymen about his being deranged, ghost-possessed or at best a fanciful poet.[152] When Mohammed had his first hallucinations of seeing the archangel Gabriel and hearing his dictation, he himself believed that he was losing

[151]The best overview of such Quranic verses is in Sita Ram Goel, ed.: *The Calcutta Quran Petition*, 3rd ed., Voice of India, Delhi 1999.

[152]Mohammed is defended against the cited qualification as "ghost-possessed" in Q.15:6, 23:70/72, 34:8, 34:46/45, 37:36/35, 44:14/13, 52:29, 68:2, 68:51, 81:22; as "a charlatan" in Q.38:4/3. In obvious reference to the arguments against Mohammed himself, earlier prophets are also said to have been called ghost-possessed: in general, Q.51:52; Noah/Nuh Q.23:25, Moses/Musa Q.26:27/26, 51:39. This way, the Quran itself testifies that Mohammed's mission was rejected by his contemporaries not because he hurt their business interests, as now commonly alleged in pop-Marxist writings, but because they greeted his supernatural claims with a healthy skepticism, the kind which pop-Marxist sources would normally endorse in the case of Hindu or Christian claims of the supernatural.

his mind, or in the parlance of the day, that he was being possessed by an evil spirit. Not to spend the rest of his life as the village idiot, he even considered committing suicide.[153] It was his wife, the self-employed and self-confident Pagan lady Khadija, who soothed him into acceptance of his pathological condition.

As modern psychology has demonstrated, Mohammed's delusion of an exceptional God-ordained vocation as God's definitive and exclusive spokesman, a delusion nourished with frequent audio-visual hallucinations (of which the verbal parts were collected to make up the Quran), was a classic case of paranoia.[154] This condition is not incompatible with worldly success, as is spectacularly exemplified by Mohammed's political and military career. But that success doesn't make his doctrine true.

The whole problem which Islam poses for its neighbours will be solved overnight if Muslims inform themselves of the deluded basis of Islam. Of course they are welcome to continue adhering to some traditions of ritual and elementary morality which their upbringing has identified with Islam; they can continue to worship Allah, a deity Mohammed borrowed from Arab Paganism; but they will see through the untenable claim that Mohammed had an exclusive telephone line with the Almighty Creator. Piecemeal solutions consisting

[153]A. Guillaume, tra.: *The Life of Muhammed, a Translation of Ibn Ishaq's Sirat Rasul Allah*, OUP, Karachi 1990 (1955), p.106/153: "I thought, Woe is me poet or possessed — Never shall Quraish say this of me! I will go to the top of the mountain and throw myself down that I may kill myself and gain rest."

[154]The most detailed and penetrating discussion of Mohammed's psychological condition is in Dr. Herman Somers: *Een Andere Mohammed*, Hadewych, Antwerp 1993; English translation forthcoming. A brief discussion is found in Maxime Rodinson: *Mohammed*, Penguin 1973 (1968), p.78-79; for this passage, the book was recently banned in Egypt. Some of its ideas were nonetheless developed further in a serial in the Egyptian magazine *Rose al-Youssef* in early 1996 by Abdullah Kamal, "A psychological analysis of prophets", which becamse the object of a fatwa; its republication in book form was prohibited and the freshly printed stock confiscated.

in communal compromises and religious harmony sop-stories may be necessary in emergency cases to save human lives; but they will not durably solve the problem of Kashmir, of the ISI's proxy war against India, of Islamic terror in numerous other countries. Only the abandonment of the defining belief of Islam, the belief in Mohammed's delusion of prophethood, can do that.

Today, more than ever before, this collective abandonment of a deluded belief is within reach. With the spread of the information revolution to the farthest corners of the desert, it need not be more difficult than the replacement of geocentrism with heliocentrism: after a handful of martyrs, it succeeded almost without effort.

1.4. GENOCIDE IN THE SUBCONTINENT

1.4.1. The Bangladesh genocide

The impression that there exists a firm resolve to deny the Hindus even their martyrs is strengthened when we consider cases of mass-slaughter of Hindus, esp. the East Bengal genocide of 1971, of which the death toll was estimated by the first Bangladesh government at 3 million.[155] Cautious researchers estimate the death toll at "one to three million" and list "Hindus" first among the targeted groups.[156] "One to three million" is exactly the range in which the death toll of the Khmer Rouge's Killing Fields is estimated, but there is just no comparison between the degree to which the Killing Fields have entered the collective consciousness (in spite of the attempt by "progressives" to downplay or

---

[155]This figure was repeated by Taslima Nasrin in an interview in *Nouvel Observateur*, 8-9-1994, and by the Bangladeshi Government in a recent bid to get Pakistan to "express regrets for the genocide against the people of Bangladesh" ("No apology for Bangladesh 'genocide'", *India Post*, 13-2-1998).

[156]Frank Chalk and Kurt Jonassohn: *The History and Sociology of Genocide*, Yale University Press, New Haven 1990, p.396.

obscure Communist crimes) and that of the East Bengali genocide. And even those who are aware that one of the biggest mass murders of the last half century took place in East Bengal, rarely realize its anti-Hindu character.

A Hindu author, Nandan Vyas, quotes Edward Kennedy and Sydney Schanberg (who monitored the 1971 events on the spot) as testifying that Hindus were the prime target of the massacre, and calculates on the basis of official demographic data that in 1971, nearly 2.5 million Hindus in East Bengal have "disappeared".[157] This figure may be exaggerated, for in spite of the Indian Government's attempt to prevent them, many East-Bengali Hindus may have managed to permanently settle in India. Still, even a lower estimate would dwarf the Muslim death toll at the hands of Hindus in post-Independence Hindu-Muslim violence. The best-kept secret of communalism-watching is that vastly more Hindus than Muslims have been killed.

Some will reply that Muslim Bengalis were also killed in 1971; true, but they were killed by West Pakistani Muslims, not by Hindus. Muslims killed in inter-Muslim clashes cannot be entered in the tally of victims fallen in Hindu-Muslim clashes. Moreover, in killing Bengali Muslims, the Pakistanis were still striking at Hinduism, not at Islam: to them, these Bengali Muslims looked too much like Hindus, wearing dhotis and saris, using a Sanskrit-based script and a sanskritized rather than arabicized vocabulary, and their ethnic separatism against a hard-won Islamic state was the best proof that their heart was not in Islam. Hindu guilt in the 1971 genocide was exactly zero. Even in the Indo-Pak war, India released the Pakistani prisoners-of-war, many of them champion rapists and Hindu-killers, all while Pakistan was killing its Indian prisoners-of-war.

The anti-Hindu character of the 1971 massacres is systematically obscured in publications by the Bangladesh

[157]Nandan Vyas: "Genocide", *Young India*, January 1995.

Government (which abandoned its initial secularism to become a full-fledged Islamic Republic in stages) as well as by Indian secularists.[158] In the absence of proper research into the exact magnitude of the 1971 massacres, it is perhaps safest provisionally to settle for a cautious estimate of half a million or so Hindus killed. This would still mean that the victims of Hindu-Muslim violence in South Asia since the Partition massacres can be divided asymmetrically in well over 90% Hindus and substantially less than 10% Muslims. Contrary to a widespread impression, the typical victim of Hindu-Muslim violence is a Hindu.

Not, of course, that this justifies any of the occasional Hindu violence, but the fact itself deserves to be noted. Indeed, to readers of the general press, it should come as a surprise: the best-kept secret about South Asia's religious conflict (not mentioned by even one recent non-Hindu author in the copious literature on the Hindu-Muslim conflict) is that the vast majority of victims consists of Hindus. Moreover, the fact that no accurate count is available, is highly significant in itself: the problem in arriving at accurate estimates is that the governments of Pakistan, India and Bangladesh (and, I am afraid, not only they) discourage serious research into the Hindu death toll in order not to foster anti-Muslim feelings. Moreover, with Pakistan being a Western ally, the powerful Anglo-American media have apparently chosen not to pay too much attention to the massacres of the East Bengali Hindus, especially in historical references afterwards (cfr. the far more numerous references to the Khmer Rouge and Rwandan "genocides"). The net result is that the victimization of Hindus remains unknown and all spotlights can be focused

---

[158]A clever way to obscure the predominantly Hindu death toll in 1971 is this circumlocution by Amit Chowdhuri (*London Review of Books*, 4-1-1996), who mentions the 1971 "genocide of the largely Muslim East Bengali population". Compare: the Jews whom Hitler killed were Europeans, most Europeans are Christians, ergo the Holocaust targeted "the largely Christian European population".

on the the sparser cases of "the poor hapless Muslim minority's misfortunes".

1.4.2. Comparison with the Holocaust

The term "genocide" begs a comparison with the Nazi Holocaust. Obviously, the genocide of Bengali Hindus was more limited in temporal and spatial extension and in technological sophistication. The percentage of the victims as compared with the total number of the targeted community was also smaller, mainly because unlike the Jews in German-occupied Europe, the Hindus in Bangladesh could flee across the border, out of their killers' reach, viz. to India. But the most interesting difference lies in the "digestion" of the memory afterwards.

One of the points of uniqueness of the Holocaust is that the victim side has not tried to make everyone forget about what happened, as survivors of such massacres usually do: "Traditionally, the victims of genocide have collaborated in the 'collective denial' by which most such events went unrecorded and/or unreported. It seemed as if the victims accepted their fate; they seemed to share the view that theirs was the lot of the weak and of the losers and was somehow ordained. The Jewish survivors of the Holocaust were the first victims of genocide to refuse to accept such a fate."[159]

The example of the Jewish Holocaust has had a certain effect on other victim groups: "Many victim groups whose survivors suffered their fate in the privacy of their hurts and their losses were amazed at the initiatives carried out by Holocaust survivors.(...) They started to publicize their fate and the injustices they had suffered by organizing publications, meetings, lobbying groups, and the commemoration of anniversaries. This clearly is not yet true of all victim groups. It is true only for those groups whose survivors take such initiatives themselves; if they do not do so,

[159]Frank Chalk and Kurt Jonassohn: *Genocide*, p.327.

the traditional silence persists and can be overcome by outsiders only with the greatest difficulty."[160] Traditionally, people don't like to be reminded of their misfortune, nor to be publicly identified with it.

In the case of the Bangladeshi Hindus, the old ways of (proud or ashamed) silence about past suffering still prevail. When I talked to a number of Hindu (Bengali) refugees in Calcutta and Varanasi, I had the "greatest difficulty" in getting them to tell their story. But that is by no means the whole explanation. There is also a remarkable non-interest in this memory on the part of the Governments concerned, and more disturbingly, there is also a blind spot regarding the genocide of Bengali Hindus among intellectuals. Thus, in the reviews of Taslima Nasreen's book *Lajja*, practically all commentators, both Western and Indian, have ignored her description of the atrocities on Hindus. Many of them falsely attributed the death sentence pronounced against her by a Mufti to her feminism, when in fact it was her drawing attention to the plight of the infidel Hindus which earned her the deadly wrath of the Islamic fanatics.[161] These commentators demonstrated on a world-wide scale the determined denial to the Hindus of even their martyrs.

The resulting ignorance or bias in public opinion is not without tangible consequences. The Jews helped foster an awareness of the history of their persecution among their former persecutors, the Christians, which makes it unlikely that Christians will target them again. A Holocaust memorial is being built in Berlin by the heirs of the *perpetrators* of the Holocaust; but there is no memorial to the massacred Hindus, because even the *victim* community doesn't bother, let alone the perpetrators. Israel's nuclear programme is accepted as a matter of course, justified by the country's genuine security concerns as proven by past victimization; but when India,

---

[160]Frank Chalk and Kurt Jonassohn: *Genocide*, p.329.

[161]Vide Koenraad Elst: postscript in Daniel Pipes: *The Rushdie Affair*, Voice of India reprint, Delhi 1998, p.294-304.

which has equally legitimate security concerns, conducted nuclear tests, it provoked American sanctions. If the world ignores Hindu security concerns, one of the reasons is that Hindus have never bothered to tell the world how many Hindus have been killed already.

1.4.3. More anti-Hindu violence

It is insufficiently realized how, even apart from the 1971 massacre, the killing of Hindus has been a frequent and large-scale affair in Pakistan and Bangladesh. In East Bengal in February 1950, "from detailed information received, the conservative estimate of casualties was placed at 2,500 killed in the district of Barisal alone. Total casualties of Dacca and East Bengal riots were estimated to be in the neighbourhood of 10,000 killed."[162] Ten days in May 1950 were enough to kill a similar number of Hindus; after this slaughter, a million Hindus fled East Pakistan within half a year.[163] For the sake of comparison: it took until the late 1980s for the total number of Muslims killed by Hindus (and the police) in post-1947 communal riots in India to reach the estimated number of 10,000.[164] Even after the wave of communal violence in 1989-93, the death toll of communal riots in independent India, including both Hindus and Muslims, had not reached 20,000 even by generous estimates.

In a survey of anti-Hindu violence in East Bengal, we may

---

[162]Muhammad Ghulam Kabir: *Minority Politics in Bangladesh*, Nawroze Kitabistan, Dhaka 1980, p.143.

[163]Bangladesh Hindu-Buddhist-Christian Unity Council: *Communal Discrimination in Bangladesh: Facts and Documents*, p.124.

[164]I am following the higher estimates here, e.g. the report on the Indian elections in *Der Spiegel*, May 1991, which assumes a figure of 12,000 *Muslim* riot victims in post-1947 India. According to P.R. Rajagopal (*Communal Violence in India*, p.16-17), who uses official police figures, the total number of people (Hindus and Muslims) killed in Hindu-Muslim riots from 1954 to 1985 was 7229. C. Jaffrelot (*The Hindu Nationalist Movement*, p.552) gives a total of some 14,000 for 1954-93, with reference to P. Brass: *Politics of India since Independence*, p.168, and to Gopal Krishna: "Communal violence in India", *Economic and Political Weekly*, 12-1-1985.

start with the Partition and the concomitant migrations. In accounts of that violent episode, the asymmetry between the Hindu and Muslim migrations is systematically overlooked. Of the Hindu and Sikh "migrants", every single one was a refugee, who was deprived of his homeland, and who would have stayed where he was had Muslims not frightened or physically driven him out. By contrast, Muslims migrated to the promised land of their own creation.[165] A large percentage of them were under no pressure at all to move, except for the promise of living in a Muslim country, and even those who had to flee (particularly in East Panjab) could have settled in safety in any other part of India rather than in Pakistan.

Consider also the numbers: of thirty million Muslims in truncated India, four million moved to Pakistan, or less than one in seven; of twenty million Hindus and Sikhs in Pakistan, seven million fled to India, or more than one in three. Moreover, in the next decade, another four million Hindus fled East Pakistan, where the situation had initially seemed less dangerous than in West Pakistan.[166] The story of the Hindu refugees is told by Prof. Saradindu Mukherji:

"No country in the world has been host to so many refugees as a 'shrinking and shrunken' India has been since the Partition in 1947. (...) According to the estimate of the Government of India, 7.30 million people entered India between 1947-51 from the two wings of Pakistan. Except a few thousand Hindu families in Sindh, almost the entire Hindu and Sikh population were forced to leave their homes. (...) In East Pakistan, the process was slow and systematic.

---

[165]Yet, *De Standaard* (Brussels, 27-6-1995: "Mohajirs oorspronkelijk vluchtelingen") explains to its readers: "Mohajirs were originally refugees". In fact *mohajir* means one who performs a *hijra*, a "migration", as Mohammed did when he left Mecca (where he was in a dead-end street, with few people feeling attracted to his message) for Medina (where he was offered a chance to establish himself and make career) in AD 622, the beginning of the Muslim calendar.

[166]Vide A.J. Kamra: *The Prolonged Partition and Its Pogroms*, Voice of India, Delhi 2000.

Between 1947-51, the total number of people moving into India was estimated at 2.55 million (...) While West Pakistan was cleansed of its Kafirs except for a microscopic minority — being reduced from 23% in 1947 to 3% at present, the non-Muslim communities of East Pakistan/Bangladesh were reduced from 29% to 12% of the population. (...)

"It is estimated that another 2.5 million Hindus fled the eastern wing of Pakistan during 1951-61. (...) One finds that 90% of the total who fled East Pakistan in course of the liberation war of Bangladesh were Hindus. (...) The extent of the missing Hindu population is estimated around 1.22 million during the period 1974-81 and about 1.73 million during the last inter-censal period of 1981-91. (...) In the Indian subcontinent, wherever the Kafirs become a minority, they are bound to become refugees, a fate which is in store for the Hindus in West Bengal, the north-eastern states and possibly Ladakh and Jammu."[167]

When looking from a distance, well-intentioned but uninformed people tend to understand conflicts in terms of the "symmetry fallacy". They think that India was divided into "Hindu India" and "Muslim Pakistan", that Hindus and Muslims both fled in the same proportion and for the same reason to the other side of the border, that Hindus in India oppress Muslims just like Muslims in Pakistan oppress Hindus. Any serious investigation of the facts blows this apparent (or projected) symmetry away. The Partition was inflicted by Muslims on Hindus, by Pakistan on India, and the balance of violence is very uneven, with a vast majority of it

---

[167]Saradindu Mukherji: "Flow of Hindu refugees from Pakistan/ Bangladesh to India: a Hindu view", *Hindustan Times*, 13-10-1996, reproduced in *Muslim India*, Jan. 1997, p.36. In a letter dd. 14-8-1996 to the Press Council, Syed Shahabuddin demanded "appropriate action" against the article as it "vilifies Islam as a religion to generate feelings of hatred and revenge against Muslim Indians and thus to aggravate communal tensions" (reproduced *ibid.*). The Press Council's reply dd. 4-11-1996 said that the matter "has been treated as closed for lack of sufficient grounds" (*ibid.*).

being inflicted by Muslims on Hindus.

As for Kashmir, where the Pakistani invaders in 1947-48 annihilated the entire Hindu presence in the part they captured, and where the communal killing in 1989-90 was equally one-sided, the subsequent killing of several thousands of Islamic terrorists and of some civilians by the Indian Army took place during two-sided armed confrontations. Even if Indian soldiers, tired of seeing their comrades ambushed and killed, have occasionally misbehaved with *mujahid* prisoners, this would still not detract from the Muslim initiative (hence guilt) in the Kashmiri conflagration. Moreover, if any innocent Muslims were killed, this was not done by any Hindu activist group, but by the multi-religious army of the secular Indian republic which emphatically rejects any tinge of Hindu identity. And here again, we should not forget that many innocent Muslim victims have been killed not by Hindus or soldiers but by other Muslims, viz. by the *mujahedin* who kidnapped girls for entertainment before dumping their dead bodies, or who shot into crowds to create the confusion needed for their own escape, or who used civilians as shields, or who tried to weed out any compromise-prone moderates or deserters. There is no Hindu guilt in any of that.

1.4.4. The "Partition Holocaust"

The "Partition Holocaust": the term is frequently used in Hindu pamphlets concerning Islam and the birth of its modern political embodiment in the Subcontinent, the state of Pakistan. Even arch-secularist Ramu Gandhi has used this terminology: "The Partition was a Holocaust, let's not forget it."[168] Is such language warranted, or is it self-ridiculing exaggeration?

The Nazi Holocaust killed the majority of European Jewry

[168]*Assignment* documentary on the BJP, presented by Nick Clarke, BBC-2, 15-6-1993. Ramu Gandhi is a grandson of Mahatma Gandhi.

and up to a quarter of the Jewish people worldwide. How many victim groups can say as much? Similar percentages apply to the Armenians in Turkey c.q. in general, and to the Tutsis in the government-controlled part of Rwanda c.q. in general (1994). The Partition pogroms, by contrast, killed hardly 0.3% of the Hindus, and though it annihilated the Hindu presence in all the provinces of Pakistan except for parts of Sindh and East Bengal, it did so mostly by putting the Hindus to flight (at least seven million) rather than by killing them (ca. half a million). Likewise, the ethnic cleansing of a quarter million Hindus from the Kashmir Valley in 1990 followed the strategy of "killing one to expel a hundred", which is not the same thing as killing them all; in practice, about 1,500 were killed. Partition featured some local massacres of genocidal type, with the Sikhs as the most wanted victims, but in relative as well as absolute figures, this does not match the Holocaust.

Among genocides, the Holocaust was a very special case, e.g. the attempt to carry it out in secrecy is unique, as is its position at the end of two millennia of constant hatred directed at the same group. It serves no good purpose to blur that specificity by extending the term to all genocides in general. Even regardless of the Holocaust uniqueness debate, the simple fact remains that the term "Holocaust" in the sense of "genocide" was chosen specifically for what the Nazis did to the Jews. Language is largely a matter of convention, and here even more than elsewhere, I think it is best to respect that convention.

A related reason why the current inflation in the use of the term *Holocaust* for contemporary mass murders (a parallel development in political discourse with the inflated use of the term *fascism*) is undesirable, is because "such elasticity in the word's range of reference can appear to trivialise the tragedy it originally designated. There may even be grounds for suspecting that the multiplication of parallels to the Judeocide is itself a form of covert anti-semitism".[169] In the case of Hindus, who are totally unconnected with and largely ignorant of Western anti-Semitism, no such design to trivialize the Holocaust is present, but it remains best to avoid making a wrong impression.

Moreover, even among Jews the term "Holocaust" is not undisputed. One reason is that originally, in the Greek translation of the Bible, *Holo-kauston*, "wholly burnt", refers to a fire-sacrifice in which the sacrificial animal is burnt completely, and which is offered by the Israelite high-priest, so that Hitler effectively gets likened to the high-priest. Therefore, many Jews prefer to use the Hebrew term *Shoah*, "disaster", instead of Holocaust. It is unwise to interfere in such sensitive matters by unthinkingly (and unaskingly) borrowing the term "Holocaust" for other purposes.

1.4.5. Genocide, the concept

If the word "Holocaust" is best avoided in describing what Muslims did to Hindus, even the more general word "genocide" does not necessarily apply to what Hinduism suffered at the hands of Islam. We will first have to investigate the matter to see if what happened really amounted to a "genocide".

To give an idea of the context of this question, we must note that the term "genocide" is used very loosely these days. One of the charges by a Spanish judge against Chilean ex-dictator Pinochet, so as to get him extradited from Great Britain in autumn 1998, was "genocide". This was his way of making Pinochet internationally accountable for having killed a few Spanish citizens: alleging a crime serious enough to overrule normal constraints based on diplomatic immunity and national sovereignty. Yet, whatever Pinochet's crimes, it is simply ridiculous to charge that he ever intended to exterminate the Spanish nation. In the current competition for victim status, all kinds of interest groups are blatantly

[169]Malcolm Bull: "One and Only", *London Review of Books*, 23/2/1995.

overbidding in order to get their piece of the entitlement to attention and solidarity. Hindus ought to do better than that.

"Genocide" means the intentional attempt to destroy an ethnic community, or by extension any community constituted by bonds of kinship, of common religion or ideology, of common socio-economic position, or of common race. The pure form is the complete extermination of every man, woman and child of the group. Examples include the complete extermination of the Native Tasmanians and many Amerindian nations from Patagonia to Canada by European settlers in the 16th-19th century. In April-May 1994, Hutu militias in Rwanda went about slaughtering the Tutsi minority, killing ca. 800,000, in anticipation of the conquest of their country by a Uganda-based Tutsi army. Though improvised and executed with primitive weapons, the Rwandan genocide made more victims per day than the Holocaust.

Hindus suffered such attempted extermination in East Bengal in 1971, when the Pakistani Army killed 1 to 3 million people, with Hindus as their most wanted target. This fact is strictly ignored in most writing about Hindu-Muslim relations, in spite (or rather because) of its serious implication that even the lowest estimate of the Hindu death toll in 1971 makes Hindus by far the most numerous victims of Hindu-Muslim violence after decolonization.

A second, less extreme type of genocide consists in killing a sufficient number who form the backbone of the group's collective identity, and assimilating the leaderless masses into the dominant community. This has been the policy the Chinese Communists in Tibet, killing over a million Tibetans while assimilating the survivors into Chinese culture by flooding their country with Chinese settlers. It was also Stalin's policy in eastern Poland and the Baltic states after they fell into his hands under the 1939 Hitler-Stalin Pact. Stalin's policies combining murder of the elites, deportation of entire ethnic groups and ruthless oppression of the survivors was prefigured in antiquity by the Assyrians, whose deportation of the ten northern (now "lost") tribes of Israel is attested in the Bible.

In antiquity, such partial genocide typically targeted the men for slaughter and the women and children for slavery or concubinage. Thus, in 416 BCE, the Athenians were angered at the Melians' reluctance to join the war against Sparta, and to set an example for other client states, Athens had Melos repopulated with Athenian colonists after killing its men and enslaving its women. Another example could be the slaughter of the Jews of Medina by Mohammed in 626 CE: after expelling two Jewish tribes, the third one, the Banu Quraiza, were exterminated: all the ca. 700 (or 900 according to another account) men were beheaded, while the women and children were sold into slavery for horses and arms, with the Prophet keeping the most beautiful woman as his concubine (she refused to marry him).

A third type of genocide consists in preventing procreation among a targeted population. Till recently, it was US policy to promote sterilization among Native American women, even applying it secretly during postnatal care or other operations. The Tibetans too have been subjected to this treatment by the Chinese Communists. In the Muslim world, male slaves were often castrated, which partly explains why Iraq has no Black population eventhough it once had hundreds of thousands of Black slaves.

A fourth type of genocide is when mass killing takes place unintentionally, as collateral damage of foolish policies, e.g. Chairman Mao's Great Leap Forward inducing the greatest man-made mass starvation killing at least 20 million, or the British war requisitions causing the Bengal famine of 1943 killing some 3 million; or as collateral damage of other forms of oppression. Unlike the deliberate genocide of Native Americans in parts of the USA or Argentina, the death of millions of Natives in Central America after the first Spanish conquests was at least partly the unintended side-effect of the hardships of forced labour and the contact with new diseases brought by the Europeans. In contrast with Nazi and Soviet work camps, where forced labour had the dual purpose of economic profit and a slow but sure death of the inmates, there is no evidence that the Spanish *wanted* their Native labourers to die. After all, their replacement with African slaves required a large extra investment.

The Atlantic slave trade itself caused mass death among the transported slaves, just as in the already long-standing Arab slave trade, but it is obvious that purely for the sake of profit, the slave-traders preferred as many slaves as possible to arrive at the slave markets alive. Likewise, the Christian c.q. Islamic contempt for Pagans made them rather careless with the lives of Native Americans, Africans or Hindus, so that millions of them were killed, and yet this was not deliberate genocide. Of course they wanted to annihilate Pagan religions like Hinduism, but in principle, the missionary religions wished to *convert* the unbelievers, and preferred not to kill them unless this was necessary for establishing the power of the 'True Faith'. While not *wanting* to kill the Pagans under their control, Christian and Muslim slave-masters were conditioned by their religion to be more careless with the lives of unbelievers than with those of believers, hence the high death toll of their non-massacres.

1.4.6. Genocide by any other name

In some cases, terminological purists object to mass murder being described as "genocide", viz. when it targets groups defined by other criteria than ethnicity. Stalin's "genocide" through organized famine in Ukraine killed some 7 million people (lowest estimate is 4 million) in 1931-33, the largest-ever deliberate mass murder in peacetime, but its victims were targeted because of their economic and political positions, not because of their nationhood. Though it makes no difference to the victims, this was not strictly genocide or "nation murder", but "class murder". Likewise, the killing of perhaps three million Cambodians by the Khmer Rouge was not an attempt to destroy the Cambodian nation; it was rather an attempt to to "purify" the nation of its bourgeois class.

Marxist apologists routinely defend their own massacres as somehow more humane than Hitler's on the specious ground that in the case of "race murder", the victim has no choice, unlike in case of "class murder" or murder for ideological reasons. As usual, the Marxists are less than truthful. In the case of class murder, no one had a choice of class the day the Communist commissars came by to round up "class enemies". Your social position on the day before, or that of your father, decided that you were a "feudal element" or a "bourgeois element", and protesting against this (generally factual) verdict only made matters worse; without any right to any kind of choice, you were made to suffer the fate preordained for the members of your designated category. In the calmer periods of Communist regimes, belonging to the wrong class no longer cost you your life, but privileges and disadvantages were still meted out on grounds of actual or hereditary class adherence, e.g. prohibiting "bourgeois" youngsters from attending university. The only choice which you could make to better your prospects, was the choice to make the Party forget your class identity by betraying more important relatives and rendering exceptional services to the regime.

In the case of murder for ideological reasons, the case is the same: the victim was targeted for something about himself that he could not control or alter by a choice of his own, viz. his convictions. A dissident was punished for publicizing his thoughts, an act which he could have chosen not to commit; but most of all he was punished for thinking the way he did, a mental act which he had not chosen. Try the test yourself: decide to think leftist if you are a rightist, and vice versa. The task is not to pretend to different opinions from the ones you hold, but to really change your heartfelt convictions by an act of will. It is as difficult as changing your race. To the expected reply that at least it was possible to hide your convictions by not telling anyone about them (which is uncertain and at any rate of little help: many Soviet citizens including professing Bolsheviks were arrested for *suspected* ideological deviations), it must be pointed out that under Nazi rule, a number of Jews likewise managed to hide their Jewishness. This achievement of concealing one's membership of the targeted category doesn't alter our moral condemnation of the latter's persecution.

The killing of large groups of ideological dissenters is a constant in the history of the monotheistic faiths, of which Marxism has been termed a modern offshoot. It started with the killing of some polytheistic priests by Pharaoh Akhenaton and, shortly after, the treacherous killing of 3,000 worshippers of the Golden Calf by Moses. They had been encouraged to come out in the open by Moses' brother Aaron, not unlike Chairman Mao's "hundred flowers" campaign which encouraged dissenters to speak freely, all the better to eliminate them later. Mass killing accompanied the christianization of Saxony by Charlemagne (ca. 800 CE) and of East Prussia by the Teutonic Knights (13th century). In 1209-29, French Catholics massacred the heretical Cathars. Wars between Muslims and Christians, and between Catholics and Protestants, killed millions both in deliberate massacres and as collateral damage, e.g. seven million Germans in 1618-48. Though the Turkish government which ordered the killing of over a million Armenians in 1915 was motivated by a mixture of purely military, secular-nationalistic and Islamic considerations, the fervour with which the local Turks and Kurds participated in the slaughter was clearly due to their Islamic conditioning of hatred against non-Muslims.

Suppose, for the sake of argument, that this ideological killing could be distinguished from genocide in the strict sense, because ethnicity was not the reason for the slaughter. While this would complicate matters for the Ukrainians or

Cambodians, it does not do so in the case of Hinduism: like the Jews, the Hindus have historically been both a religion and a nation (or at least, casteists might argue, a conglomerate of nations). Muslim attempts to kill all Hindus of a given region may therefore legitimately be termed "nation murder" or genocide.

1.4.7. Application of the term "genocide" to Hindu history

Two of the four types of genocide mentioned above have been inflicted by Muslims on the Hindus with some frequency, viz. selective extermination of the elite and off-hand mass death as a by-product of oppressive policies. Wholesale killing of all members of particular Hindu communities has occurred but only rarely. What has not been tried is a systematic attempt to prevent Hindus from procreating, eventhough the mass enslavement and deportation of Hindus to slave markets had a serious negative impact on Hindu demography.

The practice of castrating non-Muslim slaves existed in India, but only for the sake of providing eunuchs to Muslim harems, not with the deliberate purpose of destroying Hindu demography. The much-maligned Moghul emperor Aurangzeb tried to put an end to it, both because eunuchs brought endless corruption in the court and because castration was forbidden by Islamic law. In the next decades, when Islamic power collapsed, many harem eunuchs were sent away and forced to seek a new livelihood. In ancient India, harems were tended by old men or naturally *napuṁsaka*/ impotent men, tested by having to spend the night with a prostitute without showing signs of virile excitement.

The wholesale killing of all Hindus, including women and children, occasionally happened in the heat of conquest or the crushing of rebellions, but was not standard practice. Such mass killing of Hindus by Muslims rarely took place in peacetime (which does not constitute a contrast with the

Holocaust, another wartime project), but typically in the fervour immediately following military victories. However, it would be a counterproductive exaggeration to say that Muslim regimes in India entertained a design to physically exterminate the Hindus this way. Their goal was to exploit and, for the pious ones, to convert the unbelievers, and only those among the unbelievers who actively stood in the way of this project, whether as warriors or as spiritual leaders, were earmarked for slaughter.

Even during conquest, killing was usually selective. The killing of men and enslaving of women and children was standard practice in Islamic conquests. Thus, when Mohammed bin Qasim conquered the lower Indus basin in AD 712, he entered Multan and, according to the *Chach-Nâma*, "six thousand warriors were put to death, and all their relations and dependents were taken as slaves".[170] This is why Rajput women took to immolating themselves en masse to save their honour in the face of the imminent entry of victorious Muslim armies, e.g. 8,000 women immolated themselves during Akbar's capture of Chittorgarh in 1568 (where this most enlightened among Muslim rulers also killed 30,000 non-combattants). During the Partition pogroms and the East Bengali genocide, mass rape of Hindu women after the slaughter of their fathers and husbands was a frequent occurrence.

Because of India's demographic magnitude, even the selective killing of male warriors amounted to an enormous death toll, which so far no one has calculated. However, once Muslim power was established, Muslim rulers sought to convert or exploit and humiliate rather than kill the Hindus, though enforcing their rule still required a lot of small-scale but permanent terror. Even peacetime was not all that peaceful, for as Fernand Braudel wrote, Islamic rule in India as a "colonial experiment" was "extremely violent"[171], and

---

[170]H.M. Elliot and John Dowson: *The History of India as Told by Its Own Historians*, Low Price Publ., Delhi 1990 (1867), p.205.

"the Muslims could not rule the country except by systematic terror. Cruelty was the norm — burnings, summary executions, crucifixions or impalements, inventive tortures. Hindu temples were destroyed to make way for mosques. On occasion there were forced conversions. If ever there were an uprising, it was instantly and savagely repressed: houses were burned, the countryside was laid waste, men were slaughtered and women were taken as slaves."[172]

The killing of the elites in order to open up the masses to a policy of assimilation was also tried repeatedly. During the Islamic conquests in India, it was a typical policy to single out the Brahmins for slaughter, after the Hindu warrior class had been bled on the battlefield. Even the Portuguese in Malabar and Goa followed this policy in the 16th century, as can be deduced from Hindu-Portuguese treaty clauses prohibiting the Portuguese from killing Brahmins.

As for the fourth type of genocide, staggering numbers Hindus also died as collateral damage of the deliberate impoverish-ment by Sultans like Balban, Alauddin Khilji, Mohammed Tughlaq and Jahangir. As Braudel put it: "The levies [the Hindu population] had to pay were so crushing that one catastrophic harvest was enough to unleash famines and epidemies capable of killing a million people at a time. Appalling poverty was the constant counterpart of the conquerors' opulence."[173] Alauddin Khilji is hailed by secularist historians as India's first socialist, and with reason:

---

[171]Fernand Braudel: *A History of Civilizations*, Penguin 1988 (1963), p.236. That Braudel was by no means prejudiced against the Muslims may be seen from the sequel: in spite of these cruelties, "we should not be over-hasty in condemning the Muslim record in India (...) Whatever else it did, this centuries-long occupation implanted into the teeming mass of India an enormous number of faithful Muslims." Some consolation for the Hindus: for all its cruelty and destruction, Muslim rule must be credited with one major benefit to them, viz. giving them the company of an enormous number of Muslims, cut out of the flesh of Hindu society itself.

[172]Fernand Braudel: *A History of Civilizations*, p.232.

[173]Fernand Braudel: *A History of Civilizations*, Penguin 1988 (1963), p.232.

"Alauddin is notorious for having pauperized the Hindus to the utmost limit", in a deliberate policy of pushing the Hindus so deep into material hardship that they would be too busy with sheer survival to even think of rebellion.[174] While the earliest Muslim writers had described Indian prosperity, after the establishment of the Sultanate the population got impoverished, and remained so under the Moghuls: "The resultant effect of [Alauddin's] policy was that the people in the villages suffered from extreme financial hardship. The poverty of Indians was noticed in the later period by foreigners."[175]

Though all these small acts of terror added up to a death toll of genocidal proportions, no organized genocide of the Holocaust type took place. One constraint on Muslim zeal for Holy War was the endemic inter-Muslim warfare and intrigue (no history of a royal house was bloodier than that of the Delhi Sultanate and the Mughal Dynasty after Jahangir's death), another the prevalence of the Hanifite school of Islamic law in India. This is the only one among the four law schools in Sunni Islam which allows Pagans to subsist as *zimmis*, disempowered third-class citizens paying a special tax for the favour of being tolerated; the other three schools of jurisprudence ruled that Pagans, as opposed to Christians and Jews, had to be given a choice between Islam and death. This way, a compromise was effected which limited Islamic oppression to a system of ruthless exploitation which permitted the native society to survive.

Apart from actual killing, millions of Hindus disappeared

---

[174]H. Narain: *Jizyah, and the Spread of Islam*, Voice of India, Delhi 1990, p.29.

[175]K.L. Srivastava: *Position of Hindus under the Delhi Sultanate*, Munshiram Manoharlal, Delhi 1980, p.157, with reference to Francisco Pelsaert, who visited India under Jahangir: "The common people (live in) poverty so great and miserable that the life of the people can be depicted or accurately described only as the home of stark want and dwelling place of bitter woe.".

by way of enslavement. After every conquest by a Muslim invader, slave markets in Demascus, Ghazni, Bagdad and Samarkand were flooded with Hindus. Slaves were likely to die of hardship, e.g. the mountain range *Hindu Koh*, "Indian mountain", was renamed *Hindu Kush*, "Hindu-killer", when one cold night in the reign of Timur Lenk (1398-99), a hundred thousand Hindu slaves died there while on transport to Central Asia. Though Timur conquered Delhi from another Muslim ruler, he recorded in his journal that he made sure his pillaging soldiers spared the Muslim quarter, while in the Hindu areas, they took "twenty slaves each". Hindu slaves were converted to Islam, and when their descendants gained their freedom, they swelled the numbers of the Muslim community. It is a cruel twist of history that the Muslims who forced Partition on India were by and large the progeny of Hindus enslaved by Islam.

There is no official estimate of the total death toll of Hindus at the hands of Islam. A first glance at important testimonies by Muslim chroniclers suggests that, over 13 centuries and a territory as vast as the Subcontinent, Muslim Holy Warriors easily killed more than six million Hindus. The greatest among Indian Muslim historians, Ferishtha, lists several occasions when the Bahmani sultans in Central India (1347-1528) killed a hundred thousand Hindus, which they set as a minimum goal whenever they felt like "punishing" the Hindus; and they were only a third-rank provincial dynasty. The biggest slaughters took place during the raids of Mahmud Ghaznavi (1000-1026 CE); during the actual conquest of North India by Mohammed Ghori and his lieutenants (1192 ff.); and under the Delhi Sultanate (1206-1526). The Moghuls (1526-1857), even Babar and Aurangzeb, were fairly restrained tyrants by comparison. Prof. K.S. Lal once estimated that the Indian population declined by 75 million under the Sultanate, but that (or its causal relation with Islamic rule rather than with pestilence) would be hard to substantiate.[176] Research into the magnitude of the damage Islam did to India is yet to start in right earnest.

Note that attempts are made to deny this history. In Indian schoolbooks and the media, an idyllic picture of Hindu-Muslim harmony in the pre-British period is propagated in outright contradiction with the testimony of the primary sources. Like Holocaust denial, this propaganda may be called (with a continental-European term:) *negationism*. The really daring negationists don't just deny the crimes against Hindus, they invert the picture and blame the Hindus themselves. Thus, it is routinely alleged that Hindus persecuted and destroyed Buddhism; in reality, Buddhist monasteries and universities flourished under Hindu rule, but their thousands of monks were killed, their monasteries destroyed and their libraries burnt by Islamic invaders.

To quote Will Durant's famous line: "The Islamic conquest of India is probably the bloodiest story in history. It is a discouraging tale, for its evident moral is that civilization is a precious good, whose delicate complex of order and freedom, culture and peace, can at any moment be overthrown by barbarians invading from without or multiplying within."[177] The Islamic campaign against Hinduism, which has never been fully called off since the first naval invasion in 636 AD, may only occasionally have taken the form of a genocide *stricto sensu*, but considering its sheer magnitude in scope and death toll, coupled with its occasional intention to exterminate entire Hindu communities, we may deem its characterization as a "genocide" somewhat imprecise, but not really unjust.

1.4.8. Let the healing begin

---

[176]K.S. Lal: *Growth of Muslim Population in Medieval India*, Research, Delhi 1973, p.90.

[177]Will Durant: *Story of Civilization*, vol.1, *Our Oriental Heritage*, New York 1972, p.459.

What should Hindus say to Muslims when they consider the record of Islam in Hindu lands? It is first of all very important not to allot guilt wrongly. Notions of collective or hereditary guilt should be avoided. Today's Muslims cannot help it that other Muslims did certain things in 712 or 1565 or 1971. There should be no quota to keep the numbers of Muslims in certain professions down even if such quota systems exist in other countries to punish the alleged descendents of formerly privileged groups.

One thing Indian Muslims can do, however, is to critically reread their scripture to discern the doctrinal factors of Muslim violence against Hindus and Hinduism. Of course, even without scriptural injunction, people get violent and wage wars; if Mahmud Ghaznavi hadn't come, some of the people he killed would have died in other, non-religious conflicts. But the basic Quranic doctrine of hatred against the unbelievers has also encouraged many good-natured and pious Muslims to take up the sword against Hindus and other Pagans, not because they couldn't control their aggressive instincts, but because they had been told that killing unbelievers was a meritorious act. Good people have perpetrated evil because religious authorities had depicted it as good.

This is material for a no-nonsense dialogue between Hindus and Muslims. But before Hindus address Muslims about this, it is imperative that they inform *themselves* about this painful history. Apart from unreflected grievances, Hindus have so far not developed a serious critique of Islam's doctrine and historical record. Often practising very sentimental, unphilosophical varieties of their own religion, most Hindus have very sketchy and distorted images of rival religions. Thus, they say that Mohammed was an Avatar of Vishnu, and then think that they have cleverly solved the Hindu-Muslim conflict by flattering the Prophet, not realizing that it is an insult to basic Muslim beliefs which reject divine incarnation, and that it indirectly associates the Prophet with Vishnu's incarnation as a pig.

Contrary to claims made by secularist "experts" on Hindutva, fairy-tales exonerating Islam from its crimes are exactly as common among Hindu nationalists as among Gandhians. I've heard them so often in Hindutva circles: "Mohammed's message was good but later Muslims have misunderstood it", "there was communal peace until the British came to foment Hindu-Muslim enmity", "the Quran teaches tolerance but the Mullahs have misunderstood it". Instead of the silly sop stories which pass as conducive to secularism, Hindus should acquaint themselves with real history and real religious doctrines of Islam.

Another thing which we should not forget is that Islam is ultimately rooted in human nature. We need not believe the Muslim claim that the Quran is of divine origin; but then it is not of diabolical origin either, it is a human document. The Quran is in all respects the product of the mind of a 7th-century Arab businessman acquainted with and impressed by Judeo-Christian notions of monotheism and prophetism, and the good and evil elements in it are entirely human. Even its negative elements appealed to human instincts, e.g. when Mohammed promised a share in the booty of the caravans he robbed, numerous Arab Pagans took the bait and joined him. The undesirable elements in Islamic doctrine stem from human nature, and can in essence be found elsewhere as well. Keeping that in mind, it should be possible to make a fair evaluation of Islam's career in India on the basis of factual history.

I am aware that the following verdict is extremely unpopular among both politicians and intellectuals, but they should learn to face facts at last. The division of guilt for India's Hindu-Muslim conflict is extremely uneven. Hinduism may be guilty of social inequality, superstition and other evils, but intolerance of differences in religion is not one of them. It is unambiguously Islam which has brought religious persecution to India. It is Islam and Islam alone which has caused the Hindu-Muslim conflict with its many millions of mortal victims. Even when individual Hindus strike at Muslims, when they strike back once after suffering ninety-nine Islamic blows, they are merely playing a part in a drama which Islam alone has inflicted on India. The comforting implication of this seemingly harsh verdict is that it points the way to a simple and perfectly bloodless solution for the Hindu-Muslim conflict. As the Buddha said, suffering is removed by removing the cause of the suffering.